ASCENSION

LIVING BEYOND LIMITS

 **SPIRIT MEDIA**

Spirit Media Inc
https://spiritmedia.us

Spirit Media and our logos are trademarks of
Spirit Media Inc
8045 Arco Corporate Drive STE 130
Raleigh, NC 27617
1 (888) 800-3744

RELIGION | Christian Living | Spiritual Growth

Paperback ISBN: 979-8-89307-159-7
eBook ISBN: 979-8-89307-160-3
PDF ISBN: 979-8-89307-161-0

Library of Congress Control Number: 2025914996

ASCENSION

LIVING BEYOND LIMITS

BY BRYAN ELLIOTT

WITH CHANTAL FOWLER

TABLE OF CONTENTS

INTRODUCTION: BEYOND THE VEIL—YOUR JOURNEY BEGINS

WARNING: This Book May Cause Radical Transformation

Proceed with faith (and a sense of humor)!

> Caution: What you're about to read contains life-altering truths that may disrupt your current way of thinking. Side effects include: ✓ A sudden awareness of Heaven's reality all around you ✓ An irresistible hunger to experience more of God ✓ An unshakable conviction that the supernatural is meant to be normal

You've been warned. If you choose to keep reading, expect your earthly limitations to be shattered as you discover what it truly means to live an ascended life. So, buckle up and lean in—ascension isn't just a spiritual concept. It's an invitation. A way of being. A new way to see, think, and live. It's stepping into a reality where the miraculous becomes normal, where time touches eternity, and where Heaven isn't a distant hope but a present reality. You were made to ascend!

I never imagined I'd be writing a book like this. As an engineer trained in logic and rational thinking, supernatural realities weren't exactly my comfort zone. But after experiencing a profound shift in my understanding of Kingdom life, I couldn't remain silent about what I'd discovered. This journey has transformed everything for me—and it can for you too.

This understanding is firmly rooted in Scripture, particularly Ephesians 2:6 (NKJV) (NIV): "And God raised us up with Christ and seated us with him in the heavenly realms in Christ Jesus." This isn't a metaphor but our actual spiritual position. What we're exploring isn't new—it's the recovery of an ancient understanding that has been part of Christian experience since the beginning. The early Church Fathers understood this reality intimately. Maximus the Confessor wrote in his work *Centuries on Theology* (7th century, 2.88): "The Kingdom of God is within us as a potentiality now, and it will be within us as an actuality in the age to come." For Maximus and many others throughout church history, the heavenly realm wasn't just a future destination but a present reality to be experienced and manifested.

From the Desert Fathers who encountered angels and experienced divine encounters to the medieval mystics who wrote of ascending into heavenly realms, believers have always known that Heaven is accessible now. As Gregory of Nyssa expressed it in his work *On Perfection* (4th century), we are called to move "from glory to glory," progressively experiencing deeper dimensions of heavenly reality while still in this world.

? What if you could experience Heaven now?

? What if the barriers between the seen and unseen exist only in your perception?

? What if you've already been given full access, but you've been waiting for permission that was never needed?

? What if the key to the supernatural has been in your hands all along?

? What if there is more—more than you've dared to believe, more than you've been told, more than you've yet to explore?

Welcome to the adventure.

"For if we are out of our minds in a blissful, divine ecstasy, it is for God's glory. But if we are in our right minds, it is for your benefit." —2 Corinthians 5:13 (TPT)

A BIBLICAL UNDERSTANDING OF ASCENSION

Many sincere Christians hesitate when they hear terms like "ascension" or "heavenly realms," fearing these concepts belong to New Age spirituality rather than biblical Christianity. Let me address this concern directly: New Age spirituality teaches a fundamental counterfeit of biblical truth. While Scripture affirms we are made in God's image (Genesis 1:2, NKJV) and "in Him we live and move and have our being" (Acts 17:28, NKJV), New Age distorts these truths by claiming humans are inherently divine rather than created beings who reflect their Creator. It promotes self-salvation through consciousness expansion, energy manipulation, and spiritual evolution—all without need for the cross, repentance, or Jesus Christ as mediator. It typically rejects the reality of sin, denies the uniqueness of Christ, and blends spiritual practices from multiple religions into a customizable path where the self, not God, is the ultimate authority.

Many people who find themselves drawn to New Age spirituality are actually individuals with genuine spiritual gifts and sensitivities that God designed them with. These souls often have remarkable spiritual perception, prophetic inclinations, heightened empathy, or abilities to discern the spiritual atmosphere—gifts mentioned throughout Scripture as legitimate operations of the Holy Spirit (1 Corinthians 12:7-1, NKJV). Tragically, when they've sought understanding within Christian communities, many have been met with suspicion, fear, or outright rejection. Without a biblical framework to understand their experiences, they've naturally gravitated toward the only communities that validated what they were sensing—New Age circles that welcomed their gifts, albeit with distorted understanding.

The great irony is that throughout church history, from the Desert Fathers to Celtic Christianity to the Great Awakenings, the Christian faith has always included supernatural dimensions and spiritual perception. Yet in recent centuries, particularly in Western rationalistic church traditions, these aspects have been minimized or dismissed entirely. Now we're witnessing a beautiful restoration as many churches rediscover the fullness of Kingdom reality, creating safe spaces for those with spiritual sensitivities to flourish within biblical truth. When these believers find communities that embrace both sound doctrine AND supernatural experience, they often become the most effective ministers to those trapped in New Age deception—they understand the hunger that drove them there, but now carry the true satisfaction found only in Jesus Christ.

Biblical ascension, in stark contrast, is firmly rooted in Scripture—it's about awakening to the reality that, through Jesus Christ alone, believers are "seated with Him in heavenly places" (Ephesians 2:6, NKJV). Our access to heavenly realms comes exclusively through our union with Christ and His finished work on the cross. The Bible itself is filled with accounts of believers experiencing spiritual realities: Paul was "caught up to the third heaven" (2 Corinthians 12:2—4, NKJV), John was invited to "come up here" to witness heavenly visions (Revelation 4:1, NKJV), Stephen saw "heaven opened" as he was being martyred (Acts 7:55—56, NKJV), and countless others throughout church history have testified to divine encounters and heavenly experiences.

The enemy's strategy has always been to create counterfeits of God's genuine spiritual gifts and experiences. Satan—who is utterly defeated through Christ's finished work on the cross—now only retains the power of deception. By promoting these distorted versions of spiritual truth, he attempts to dissuade believers from embracing the supernatural inheritance God has prepared for us. He knows that when Christians walk in the fullness of their heavenly position in Christ, his already broken influence diminishes even further. What I'm inviting you into isn't new or foreign to Christian faith—it's the recovery of an inheritance that has always belonged to every believer through Jesus Christ.

But perhaps this story will illustrate the difference more clearly than theological explanations can:

Proceed with bold love (and maybe a few laughs).

Let's be clear: this isn't "New Age"—though it might feel new, radical, and full of radiant light. It's the oldest truth the world knows—Jesus, alive, and well, walking through Santa Cruz with sandals, a smile, and a few divine appointments lined up.

I was just outside of Santa Cruz one weekend after a Kingdom transformation conference, ready for two chill days of coffee, ocean air, and down time. But as we pulled into Santa Cruz, a few spiritually sensitive friends immediately noted, "Whoa... the atmosphere feels dark here." I had overheard stories about satanic temples in the hills, strange energies, and Buddhas on every street corner.

And I'll admit—part of me wanted to simply return to our original plan of relaxation. But then something stirred in me. Wait a second. Didn't I just come from a conference on transformation? If I carry His light, why wouldn't I expect it to shine the brightest in places that seem the darkest?

So I did what any sane Kingdom agent would do: I went shopping. Bought a stack of books like Jesus Calling and Daily Meditations with Jesus, and made a mission out of it.

At the hotel check-in desk, the woman who gave me my room key ended up giving her heart to Jesus after a few minutes spent getting to know her and sharing the gospel. Just like that.

At the coffee shop? Conversations turned to Christ.

At restaurants? Servers let me pray with them—one even received a devotional through tears.

On the street? I met a homeless transgender man, formerly involved in Satanism, completely hopeless. But he let me pray for him and, lay hands on him, and he walked away holding *Jesus Calling*, with hope in his eyes that hadn't been there before.

You see, people in New Age spaces are often spiritually sensitive and genuinely seeking. They're hungry for authentic spiritual reality. They are spiritually awake, searching for something more. They're not offended by Jesus. In fact, they're often intrigued. Because when religion has failed them and performance-based living has left them burned out, they are ready—wide open—for real love, real freedom, and real life. His name is Jesus.

Religion says: "Try harder, be better, earn it." It's stuffy, rigid, and rule-obsessed—focusing on outward behavior while neglecting the heart. Traditional religion often actively avoids supernatural experiences, viewing them with suspicion or fear. It creates systems that feel devoid of life and wonder, offering little that would genuinely attract spiritual seekers. This fear-based approach emphasizes what to avoid rather than what to embrace, leaving people hungry for real connection with the divine.

Jesus says: "You've been known since before time began. You are fully loved, fully forgiven, fully free. Heaven is within. Welcome home." He offers a relationship, not religion—vibrant experience, not empty ritual.

The truth is, what many call "New Age" is often just unredeemed hunger for truth wrapped in crystals and incense. But the Gospel? It's the fulfillment of every spiritual longing. The Kingdom doesn't compete with spiritual seekers' hunger—it fulfills what they're truly searching for with the authentic reality found only in Christ. Not as a counterfeit, but as the original.

We're not here to judge—we're here to love. We don't run from dark-ness—we light it up. That's what Jesus did. That's what sons and daughters do.

So next time you find yourself surrounded by "spiritual seekers," re-member: the veil is already thin. The harvest is ripe. And Heaven is always within reach.

A NOTE ABOUT EMOJIS

You'll notice emojis throughout these books—they're authentically how I communicate! ☺ When I once sent text messages without them, my spiritual operations team immediately checked if I was okay! Emojis add expressions where plain text falls short, break up dense para-graphs, and bring light to serious topics.

A Note on Terminology: Transformation and Awakening

Throughout this book, I use terms like "transformation," "revealing," "unveiling," and "awakening" when discussing our spiritual journey in Christ. This reflects an important biblical truth: In Christ, we are not be-coming something foreign to God's plan, but rather growing into what He always intended us to be. New creation life, resurrected life was al-ways God's original design for humanity. Through Christ's finished work on the cross, we don't just receive a temporary fix—we are restored to our true identity as sons and daughters of God, living from the reality of His Kingdom within us. As we embrace this truth, we begin to experi-ence the fullness of what Jesus meant when He said, "I have come that they may have life, and that they may have it more abundantly" (John 10:10, NKJV).

When Paul writes in Colossians 3:3-4 (TPT), "Your crucifixion with Christ has severed the tie to this life, and *now* your true life is hidden away in God in Christ. And as Christ himself is seen for who he really is, who you really are will also be revealed, for you are *now* one with him in his glory!" he points us to a wonderful truth. As we grow in our understanding of Jesus, we also grow in understanding our identity in Him—we are one with Him in His glory right **NOW!**

This perspective is key to understanding the life of faith described in this book. We're not trying to earn a new identity through religious effort. The changes happening in us aren't creating something entirely new—they're bringing to light what God established in Christ before the foundation of the world (Ephesians 1:4, NKJV). This truth appears throughout Scripture: we are complete in Christ (Colossians 2:10, NKJV), blessed with every spiritual blessing (Ephesians 1:3, NKJV), made righteous through Him (2 Corinthians 5:21, NKJV), and given everything we need for godly living (2 Peter 1:3, NKJV).

So when you read about transformation in these pages, understand it as growing into your true identity in Christ—removing the barriers that have prevented you from seeing who you are in Him. This isn't just a change in words but a fundamental shift in how we understand our faith journey: we are growing into who God has always seen us to be.

Jesus' declaration from the cross—"It is finished!" (John 19:30, NKJV)—was a complete victory, establishing our new life, our oneness with God, and placing His Kingdom within us. The cross didn't create this reality—it revealed it. Your journey isn't about becoming someone else but growing into the person God created you to be in Christ.

THE KINGDOM AT HAND

In these pages, I invite you to explore ascension and the kingdom within—living from our seated position with Christ in heavenly places while still walking on earth. As an engineer, I never imagined writing about spiritual realms, yet my journey has taken me beyond what I once thought possible. Some perspectives may stretch traditional frameworks, and that's okay. You're welcome to test these ideas, question them, and take only what resonates. My hope isn't that you agree with everything, but that together we might glimpse the fullness of our inheritance in Christ, where Heaven and earth converge in our daily lives.

? What if Heaven isn't somewhere far away, but fully accessible right now?

? What if your spirit already knows how to engage with the realms of God, but your mind just hasn't caught up yet?

? What if ascension isn't about escaping this world but bringing Heaven into it—through you?

Let me be clear about what I mean by "ascension." In simple terms, ascension is the practice of living from your true position in Christ—seated with Him in heavenly places—while still walking on earth. It's awakening to the reality that Heaven is your native realm and learning to function from that awareness in your everyday life. It's not about creating a new connection to God—it's about recognizing the connection that has always existed and living from that place of union.

This understanding resonates deeply with what Teresa of Ávila described in her *Interior Castle* (1577, p. 42), where she mapped out the soul's journey into ever-deepening communion with God—not as a distant hope but as an experiential reality. She taught that the innermost dwelling place, where we experience complete union with God, wasn't reserved for the afterlife but was accessible here and now to those who followed the path of surrender and love.

Many believers feel disconnected from heavenly realities because they've been taught that intimacy with God is something to strive for rather than something to wake up to.

? What if that disconnect isn't because Heaven is distant, but because we haven't recognized how near it truly is?

? What if the veil between Heaven and earth that once seemed so impenetrable was completely removed at the cross, and now we're simply learning to see what has always been available?

As Athanasius boldly declared in his work *On the Incarnation* (4th century, ch. 54), "God became man so that man might become god." This stunning statement—echoed by numerous church fathers—wasn't suggesting we become divine in essence, but that we participate in divine nature through our union with Christ, experiencing the realities of Heaven even while on earth.

This book is an invitation into the ascended life—a life where we walk in the fullness of our identity as sons and daughters of God, where we no longer live under the weight of earthly limitations, and where we embrace our divine calling as co-heirs with Christ.

We will explore:

The reality of ascension—what it means to live from above while walking on earth

How to engage with heavenly realms—stepping into the supernatural as your normal

Your true authority as a believer—unlocking Kingdom realities now, not someday

The power of divine union with Christ—living from oneness, not striving for it

"At last the fulfillment of the age has come! It is time for the realm of God's kingdom to be experienced in its fullness!" —Mark 1:15 (TPT)

Through Christ's incarnation and resurrection, every false boundary between Heaven and earth, the sacred and the secular, the mystical and the theological, the supernatural and the natural has been erased forever.

What humanity once perceived as separation was never real—only a veil of misunderstanding. The veil has been torn.

Now, in Christ, the fullness of God's presence is revealed in all things, inviting us to live in the seamless reality of His Kingdom, here and now!

BREAKING THROUGH LIMITATIONS

? What if everything Jesus said is literally true—and not just for some future time, but for right now?

? What if Heaven isn't waiting for you, but you're the one who needs to wake up to where you already are?

? What if everything that seems impossible is only an illusion created by unbelief?

? What if you are already seated with Christ in heavenly places (Ephesians 2:6, NKJV, NIV) and learning to ascend is simply becoming aware of where you actually are in Him?

"And God raised us up with Christ and seated us with him in the heavenly realms in Christ Jesus." —Ephesians 2:6 (NKJV) (NIV)

This truth was profoundly understood by Cyril of Alexandria who wrote in his *Commentary on John* (5th century, Book I), "Christ did not ascend alone, but we also ascended with Him. For since He comes from us, from our nature... we are all in Christ." The early church didn't see our heavenly position as metaphorical but as an ontological reality—the very foundation of our Christian experience.

? What if your spirit is designed to move freely between realms just like Philip in Acts, who was instantly transported by the Spirit (Acts 8:39—40, NKJV)?

Throughout Christian history, saints have experienced this reality. Bernard of Clairvaux described in his *Sermons on the Song of Songs* (12th century, Sermon 71) moments when "the Word and the soul became one spirit," enabling believers to transcend natural limitations. Brother Lawrence practiced what he called "the sacrament of the present moment"—a continuous awareness of heavenly reality permeating everyday activities, as recorded in The Practice of the Presence of God (17th century, Fourth Conversation).

? What if miracles, encounters, and heavenly realities were never meant to be rare, but your daily experience?

? What if the Kingdom of Heaven is already inside you (Luke 17:21, NKJV, TPT), and your job is not to strive for it but to unlock and manifest it?

"The kingdom of God is not discovered in 1 place or another, for God's kingdom realm is already expanding within some of you." —Luke 17:21 (TPT)

The Desert Fathers understood this profoundly. As Abba Anthony said in the Sayings of the Desert Fathers (4th century), "The kingdom of heaven is within you; and whoever knows and loves himself discovers that treasure." This wasn't abstract theology—it was practical spirituality that transformed how they lived in the world.

🔥 The Kingdom of God is Jesus Himself! This Kingdom resides within us, continually unfolding in and through our lives.

🔥 God is in us, and we are in Him. He will never be closer or further away than He is right now; we simply awaken more fully to the reality of our union with Him.

🔥 All that's required is a simple shift of consciousness—moving from sin-consciousness to Christ-consciousness, which is a biblical awareness of our identity in Christ and His finished work, rather than focusing on our shortcomings. This shift helps us live from the spirit while on earth.

? What if the supernatural isn't reserved for the "spiritually elite," but is your birthright as a child of God?

Origen of Alexandria taught in his *On First Principles* (3rd century, Book I, ch. 1) that every believer possesses "spiritual senses" that can be awakened through communion with God. These senses—spiritual sight, hearing, taste, touch, and smell—enable us to perceive and interact with heavenly realities. This teaching wasn't considered extraordinary but fundamental to Christian formation.

? What if time itself bends in the presence of eternity, and you could step into divine moments outside the limits of earthly constraints?

Hildegard of Bingen, the 12th-century mystic, experienced what she called "the living Light" where her spirit would receive divine communications that transcended normal time and space. In her work *Scivias* (1151, Book I, Vision 1), she wrote, "Heaven was opened and a fiery light of exceeding brilliance came and permeated my whole brain." These weren't just private visions but encounters that transformed her community and continue to inspire believers today.

? What if ascension is not a gift for a few but an invitation for all—one that is waiting for you to simply say yes?

YOUR DIVINE INVITATION

This is more than just a book—it's a disruption to the way you've been taught to think about life, faith, and what's possible.

Jesus didn't come to establish another religion—He came to reveal the Kingdom. And this Kingdom isn't waiting for you on the other side of death—it's waiting for you to wake up to it now.

Ascension is the practice of living from your heavenly position—a position you've always had through the finished work of the cross, but perhaps haven't fully recognized or experienced in your daily life.

John of the Cross described this invitation in *The Ascent of Mount Carmel* (1579, Book II, ch. 8) as "the secret ladder, disguised," by which the soul ascends to divine union. This path isn't complicated, but it does require a willingness to let go of old mindsets and embrace a new way of seeing. As Meister Eckhart boldly declared in his *Sermons* (14th century, Sermon 6), "God is at home. It is we who have gone out for a walk." Our journey isn't about reaching a distant destination but returning to what has always been our true home.

⁘ Everything you've ever needed has already been given.

⁘ Everything you long for is already available.

⁘ The veil has been torn, the door is open, and the invitation has already been sent.

Will you step through?

This is the invitation to ascend—not someday, not when you "arrive" spiritually, but today.

It's time to think differently. It's time to see differently. It's time to live differently.

☞ *Are you ready? Then let's go up.*

THE GOOD NEWS OF INNOCENCE: THE KEY TO ASCENSION

"So don't ever be afraid, dearest friends! Your loving Father joyously gives you His kingdom with all its promises!" —Luke 12:32 (TPT)

❓ What if the Kingdom was first freely received, and that receiving ignites our passionate pursuit?

❓ What if innocence—our original, uncorrupted state—was already restored in Christ, awakening a hunger for its fullness?

❓ What if knowing we are already loved and accepted is what activates the faith of God within us?

The concept of restored innocence echoes what Isaac the Syrian wrote in his *Ascetical Homilies* (7th century, Homily 51): "Sin, Gehenna, and death do not exist at all with God, for they are effects, not substances. Sin is the fruit of free will. There was a time when sin did not exist, and there will be a time when it will not exist." This profound insight reveals that our true nature—our original innocence—was never truly lost but only obscured, and in Christ is fully restored.

🔥 It is our Father's delight—His joy—to give us His Kingdom! Not as a future reward, not as something we work to attain, but as a present inheritance, freely given and fully accessible.

🔥 This is not an invitation to escape earth, but to live fully from Heaven while still here.

When we truly receive the revelation that we are loved, accepted, and valued by God, the faith of God awakens within us. This divine gift—not our human striving—is what transforms our hearts.

It is the full outpouring of His love—a Kingdom so rich in grace and overflowing with promise that it leaves no room for fear, striving, or insufficiency.

There is no longer any separation, for the finished work of Jesus has abolished religion and performance-based living.

It is finished.

We are gloriously free, forgiven, and victorious by the gift of grace received through faith. There is absolutely nothing we can add to the cross or to the total victory of Jesus. Our own righteousness amounts to nothing; the grace of God is the free gift that has everything to do with Jesus and nothing to do with our performance. Sin's authority has been stripped, death has been conquered, and we now live as heirs of a triumphant Kingdom, secure in the finished work of Christ. Jesus is infinitely above all the combined forces of rule, authority, dominion, and government—He towers head and shoulders above everything, and we are seated with Him in that reality (Ephesians 2:6, NKJV, NIV).

? If this is true, then why do we still live as if we are waiting for access, when Heaven has already flung the doors wide open?

Through Christ, we are forever blameless and innocent, restored to our original design. The work is complete, the victory assured, and our inheritance secured. Ascension is not about going somewhere—it's about waking up to where you already are and what is within. We are invited to live not in the shadow of what could be but in the fullness of what already is—a Kingdom freely given, fully established, and eternally unshakable.

🔥 The Kingdom of God is not a distant land, not an ethereal afterlife. The Kingdom is a Person. Jesus Christ. And He lives in you.

🔥 You are His dwelling place, His throne, His gateway into the world.

Gregory of Nyssa captured this reality when he wrote in *The Life of Moses* (4th century, Book II, para. 244), "The goal of our journey is not to arrive at a place but to become like the One we seek." The Kingdom is not primarily a location but a state of being—awakening to our divine life manifested through human vessels.

? Have you ever wondered why Jesus told us to pray, "Your Kingdom come, Your will be done, on earth as it is in Heaven" (Matthew 6:10, NIV)?

Not one day, not eventually, but now. He never taught us to wait for the Kingdom—He taught us to release it. To manifest it. To bring it. If Heaven is within you, then what's stopping you from living from that reality today?

The gospel of the Kingdom is more astonishingly incredible than we can fully comprehend. It is an announcement so liberating that it breaks every chain of bondage and severs every tie to religion and performance-based living. It is received by faith, not achieved. Through the fall, humanity was bound to an earthly existence, but in Christ, we are awakened to our new creation reality in union with Jesus—a redeemed, heavenly life of oneness where the distortion of sin no longer defines us.

Ascension is the practice of remembering. Of seeing through the illusion of limitation and separation. It is living from a place of rest and trust, allowing our minds to align with the truth of our spirits. We are awakening to righteousness, to our shared likeness of Christ and redeemed innocence, free from the effects of sin, reflecting the image of God in which we were created. We are complete in Christ. There is nothing left to earn, nothing left to wait for, nothing outside of us that we lack. We now live overwhelmed with God's opinion of us—beloved sons and daughters, kings and priests, royal ambassadors and prisoners of love, fully backed by Heaven.

THE SUPREMACY OF CHRIST: THE FOUNDATION OF ALL CREATION

When exploring the mystical aspects of our faith, it's essential to ground everything in the absolute supremacy of Christ. Colossians 1 gives us one of the most profound declarations of Christ's centrality to all creation found anywhere in Scripture. Let's examine how this foundational truth serves as the bedrock for our understanding of ascension and heavenly realities.

THE COSMIC CHRIST: CREATOR AND SUSTAINER OF ALL THINGS

Colossians 1:15-20 presents a breathtaking portrait of Jesus:

"Christ is the visible image of the invisible God. He existed before anything was created and is supreme over all creation, for through him God created everything in the heavenly realms and on earth. He made the things we can see and the things we can't see—such as thrones, kingdoms, rulers, and authorities in the unseen world. Everything was created through him and for him. He existed before anything else, and he holds all creation together. Christ is also the head of the church, which is his body. He is the beginning, supreme over all who rise from the dead. So he is first in everything. For God in all his fullness was pleased to live in Christ, and through him God reconciled everything to himself. He made peace with everything in heaven and on earth by means of Christ's blood on the cross." —Colossians 1:15-20 (NLT)

This passage establishes several crucial truths:

- Christ is the perfect image of God — When we see Jesus, we see exactly what God is like

- Christ pre-existed creation — He wasn't created; He was the Creator

- All things were created through Him — Nothing exists apart from His creative power

- All things were created for Him — The purpose of all creation is Christ Himself

- He holds all creation together — The very fabric of the universe depends on Him moment by moment

- He is the head of the church — His authority extends over all believers

- He reconciled all things to God — His work of restoration extends to the entire cosmos

This comprehensive vision of Christ's supremacy forms the foundation for understanding our ascension experiences and heavenly engagement.

FROM THE UNIVERSAL TO THE PERSONAL

From the very beginning, God's heart overflowed with relentless love—not just for a select few, but for the entire cosmos ("For God so loved the world [kosmos]" —John 3:16, NIV).

This means every person, every living creature, and all creation throughout the universe is cherished beyond measure.

To powerfully demonstrate the magnitude of this love, He freely gave His only begotten Son, Jesus, who entered our human experience to awaken us to our original identity and eternal union with Him.

In giving us Jesus, God extended a stunning invitation: Whoever believes—meaning whoever awakens through faith to the truth of their restored innocence and inclusion in Christ—steps out of the illusion of separation and into the vibrant reality of eternal life. Yet, even this faith is not something we generate through our own striving or effort; it is the very faith of God imparted within us, as Galatians 2:20 beautifully expresses, "I live by the faith of the Son of God, who loved me and gave Himself for me" (KJV).

Through Christ, God has called us into a life of breathtaking freedom—a freedom not earned but joyously given. We know our own righteousness amounts to nothing; there is nothing we can add to the gift of salvation. Innocence is not something we work toward—it is something we awaken to. This profound revelation removes all striving, empowering us to restfully receive and effortlessly live out our true identity in Him.

COSMIC RECONCILIATION: OUR INVITATION INTO ASCENSION

Colossians 1:19-20 beautifully unveils the breathtaking scope of Christ's reconciling work:

"For God is satisfied to have all his fullness dwelling in Christ. And by the blood of his cross, everything in heaven and earth is brought back to himself—back to its original intent, restored to innocence again!" — Colossians 1:19-20 (TPT)

This scripture isn't merely poetic theology; it reveals the stunning, transformative reality at the heart of the gospel—the cosmic reconciliation fully accomplished through Christ's blood shed on the cross. Pay close attention: "everything" has been restored—both earthly and heavenly

29

realms. The blood of Jesus isn't a distant hope, conditional promise, or something we strive to access through religious effort; it's the definitive declaration of our restored innocence and union with God.

Imagine for a moment that the veil between Heaven and earth hasn't just been thinned; it's been utterly torn apart through Christ's victorious sacrifice. The fullness of God—His complete divine essence—dwelt fully in Jesus, and through Him, peace and original intent have been established across every realm of existence.

LIVING FROM THE REALITY: A NEW PERSPECTIVE: ASCENSION AS AWAKENING

The finished work of Jesus on the cross radically transforms everything:

⁖ The heavenly realms are now accessible through Him—we enter into heavenly experiences because Christ has fully opened the way.

⁖ Our seated position with Him is secure—we don't ascend through religious striving or rituals; we awaken to the truth that we're already seated with Him in heavenly places (Ephesians 2:6, TPT).

⁖ Our authority flows from His absolute authority—not from religious performance, but from the glorious truth that every dominion and power has already been subjected to Christ's victorious reign.

⁖ Our identity is anchored in His unchanging nature—our true self is revealed in the mirror of Christ's perfect reflection, free from distortions of religious striving and performance-based spirituality.

⁖ Our ability to ascend is based solely on His reconciling work—ascension isn't a spiritual achievement or a merit-based reward; it's a beautiful awakening to the eternal reality of our union with Christ.

A NEW PERSPECTIVE: ASCENSION AS AWAKENING

When Christ declared, "It is finished" (John 19:30, NIV), He proclaimed the end of separation, the abolition of religious striving, and the full establishment of divine union. This cosmic reconciliation removes the illusion that Heaven is distant and inaccessible. Instead, Heaven is vividly present, just a breath away, accessible as we awaken to the truth of our eternal identity in Christ.

As Francois du Toit beautifully shares in the *Mirror Study Bible* (2012, p. 18), the gospel doesn't offer potential forgiveness—it proclaims fully accomplished redemption. We aren't waiting to be reconciled; we're awakening to our eternal reconciliation already secured at the cross.

Ascension, therefore, becomes not a quest for higher spiritual experiences but a joyful recognition of what is already ours in Christ. The throne—room of Heaven is wide open, inviting us to boldly approach and fully experience the wonders of our divine inheritance (Hebrews 4:16, TPT).

LIVING FROM UNION WITH THE SUPREME CHRIST

When we understand the supremacy of Christ, we recognize that ascension isn't about reaching a distant God but about awakening to our union with the One who is already "above all things" while simultaneously "in all things" (Colossians 3:11, NIV).

This transforms how we approach the ascended life:

◆ We don't strive to reach heavenly places—we recognize we're already seated there with Christ

◆ We don't work to earn divine communion—we rest in the union Christ has already secured

◆ We don't beg for access to divine wisdom—we draw from the One in whom "all the treasures of wisdom and knowledge" are hidden (Colossians 2:3, NIV)

The practice of ascension is simply the practical outworking of the truth Paul proclaims in Colossians 3:3-4:

"For you died, and your life is now hidden with Christ in God. When Christ, who is your life, appears, then you also will appear with him in glory." —Colossians 3:3-4 (NIV)

Our life is already "hidden with Christ in God." Ascension is the practice of aligning our awareness with this reality, allowing us to operate from our true position in Him.

What If...?

？ What if your entire understanding of reality was transformed by truly comprehending Christ's supremacy?

？ What if every ascension experience was simply an awakening to where you already are in Him?

？ What if the One who holds all creation together is inviting you into deeper awareness of His indwelling presence right now?

This is the invitation before you—not to reach for something distant, but to awaken to the reality of union with the supreme Christ who has reconciled all things to Himself and who holds your very life within His own.

CHAPTER 1: ✦⋅💧 A DIVINE CONVERGENCE

FAITH, ENGINEERING, AND MYSTICAL ENCOUNTERS

What happens when you mix the Holy Spirit, a super technical, entrepreneurial, and logical engineer, and an on-fire French mystic housewife and worship leader who both love Jesus? You get a Kingdom invasion! You witness the practice of ascension—living from heavenly places while walking on earth—unfolding through unlikely partnerships as Heaven's reality breaks forth through ordinary people.

This divine convergence isn't new to Christian history. Throughout the ages, God has brought together unexpected collaborators to manifest His Kingdom. As Symeon the *New Theologian*, an 11th-century Byzantine mystic, wrote: "The Kingdom of Heaven is neither far from us nor near; it is within us." When unlikely partners unite in the pursuit of heavenly realities, the Kingdom manifests in remarkable ways.

Now imagine what will happen as the entire body of Christ awakens to the profound reality of our oneness. Imagine diverse streams, traditions, cultures, and generations flowing together as one unstoppable river of divine love. Imagine barriers dissolving, divisions healed, and unity arising effortlessly—not through human striving, but through collective awakening to our shared identity in Christ. Imagine the power, creativity, and transformative impact released when we align as one heart, one purpose, and one family. This is the divine convergence we stand on the threshold of, where Heaven fully invades earth and God's Kingdom is manifest like never before!

This is the great awakening that is underway on the earth!

BRYAN'S JOURNEY: FROM LOGIC TO THE SUPERNATURAL

My name is Bryan Elliott. Above all else, I'm a beloved son of God, deeply cherished by my Father, passionately captivated by Jesus, and sustained by the grace of my life—union with Him. I'm also a husband, a father, an engineer, an entrepreneur, and a man whose journey has been marked by both struggle and extraordinary redemption.

Before I share my story, I want you to know that what follows isn't the account of someone who's always been "spiritually sensitive" or naturally attuned to the supernatural. In fact, quite the opposite. As an engineer trained in concrete facts and empirical evidence, I approached faith primarily through logic and reason for most of my life. What I'm about to share represents a journey that surprised me more than anyone.

When the apostle Paul wrote that "God chose the foolish things of the world to shame the wise" (1 Corinthians 1:27), I never imagined I'd be living proof of that scripture. But God, in His wisdom and humor, often uses the most unlikely people to demonstrate His truths. If He can reveal these realities to someone as analytically minded and spiritually reserved as I once was, imagine what He might reveal to you.

My story isn't about achievements or titles. It's a journey of awakening—a beautiful unfolding revelation that my identity has never been defined by my past, my performance, or my limitations. Instead, my identity flows directly from my eternal union with Christ, a profound reality I'm still joyfully discovering each day.

I've come to see that the true gospel isn't a call to religious performance but the unveiling of what has always been true about us—our redeemed innocence, our inclusion in God's family, and our complete reconciliation, fully accomplished by Jesus. This gospel hasn't merely shifted my perspective; it has reshaped the very fabric of my life.

As I awaken more deeply to this divine union, I'm entering a place of rest that surpasses understanding, freed from every false identity that once held me captive. Now, from this place of peace, I'm no longer striving to become something new but joyfully revealing who I've always been: fully loved, fully accepted, fully alive in Him.

I was born into a multi-generational Christian family, yet our home experienced trauma and tragedy that marked us significantly for many years. By the age of eighteen, I had never had a meaningful spiritual experience. Jesus made sense logically, but my heart was full of wounds that I never addressed, leaving me emotionally disconnected.

🔥 "For too long, I lived with a head knowledge of God but a heart that remained untouched by His presence."

This disconnect wasn't because God was distant—He was always present. The barrier was in my perception, not in reality. Like the ancient mystic Gregory of Nyssa once wrote, "The Divine Being is bound-less and incomprehensible" (*Life of Moses*, 4th century, Book II.163). I wasn't experiencing God not because He was hiding, but because I wasn't yet awakened to His ever-present reality.

Driven by pride and rebellion, I left the faith and chose to live life on my own terms. Though I believed in Jesus theoretically, my life didn't reflect His Kingdom. Over the next few decades, I slowly inched back to God, but I still had one foot in the world.

For many years, I was stuck in a mindset of knowledge and logic, while my emotions were on lockdown. It wasn't until 2016, when I finally sur-rendered and made God the Lord of my life, that everything began to change. Healing started to take place, and my heart came alive. Finally, I stepped into the realm of the Kingdom, a reality that was completely foreign to me for forty-six years.

Reflection Questions:

? Have you ever felt the disconnect between what you know about God intellectually and what you've experienced of Him personally?

? What might be keeping you from fully surrendering to the reality of God's Kingdom?

Never in a million years would I have imagined writing a book like this or even pondering such big, bold questions about faith and the truth of God's Word. But if God could do this for me—someone who had never experienced anything spiritual and was disconnected from his emo-tions—He can do it for anyone. If God can awaken me after so long, I truly believe He can awaken anyone willing to receive.

Looking back, I can see God's hand at work in my life. The deep losses, the suffering, the brokenness—they were all part of a journey that led me to truly understand the "Now and Not Yet" of God's Kingdom. Through it all, I have learned that God's Kingdom is not just a future hope—it is here, right now, and we can live in its fullness daily through the practice of ascension.

This journey from intellectual understanding to spiritual experience mirrors what Origen of Alexandria called "the ascent of the mind to God"—a progression from mere mental knowledge to direct spiritual encounter. For Origen, true knowledge of God came not through reasoning alone but through the purification of the heart and the illumination of the spirit (*On First Principles*, 3rd century, Book IV, ch. 3.11).

ENTER CHANTAL: HEAVEN'S GATEWAY

I first met Chantal in January 2016 when I made Jesus Lord of my life and started a prayer team for my business, Flō Energy Solutions Inc. Back then, I didn't know the Word of God, my life still had a lot of mixture, and the heavenly realm was not something I had ever experienced. I had never even prayed out loud before and didn't plan to join the prayer team I enlisted for my company, but the conviction of the Holy Spirit pushed me forward.

Today, Chantal is a dear friend and the director of Flō's spiritual operations team. At Flō, we operate as a Kingdom company, deeply committed to honoring God's principles by intentionally integrating various forms of prayer and spiritual intelligence into every aspect of our daily operations. Recognizing there is no separation between sacred and secular, we have dedicated team members whose primary role is actively listening to God's voice, living from a lifestyle of ascension—engaging daily with heavenly realms, seeing God in everything, and continually awakening our company to the fullness of His Kingdom reality.

This integration of spiritual practice into business life reflects what the medieval Benedictines understood through their motto "ora et labora" (prayer and work). They recognized that work itself could be sanctified and become a vehicle for spiritual transformation when done in the context of prayer and divine communion (*The Rule of St. Benedict*, 6th century, Chapter 48).

Chantal has played a pivotal role in accelerating my journey into the practice of ascension. Her deep faith and guidance have been instrumental in opening my heart to new dimensions of spiritual realities, teaching me the power of focusing on heavenly things while living fully on earth. Through her mentorship, I began to understand that the supernatural is not some distant concept but a present reality we are called to engage with every day, pulling Heaven into the now.

Chantal's testimony unlocked new depths of faith and spiritual understanding for me. She showed me that ascension is more than just an experience—it's a lifestyle of living from heaven's perspective. Her journey revealed the invitation for all of us to step into the heavenly realms, to move from glory to glory, and to bring the reality of Heaven into our everyday lives.

CHANTAL'S STORY: FROM DREAMS TO DIVINE ASSIGNMENTS

In Chantal's own words:

I never thought I would find myself in this place—writing about my life and co-authoring a book.

It is said that it takes a whole tapestry of people to bring you to where you are today. I can testify to that truth. We cannot do this journey on our own, and I am deeply grateful for every person God has brought into my life and for the places where He has planted me so I could grow.

I've lived most of my life quietly and simply. Writing my story was never something I pursued, but my friend Bryan persistently asked me to submit some of my stories for a new project he was working on. At first, I felt challenged. I wasn't prepared to release those spiritual experiences for such a time as this. As I questioned God about it, He began to tell me that not only would I submit my stories, but I would also share my testimony—and I was not to hold back.

I had countless reasons to disqualify myself from participating, but Bryan's persistence and God's prompting kept pulling me forward. After hearing from the Lord and submitting my stories bit by bit, one of Bryan's editors suggested I co-author the book with him. It was a confirmation of what God had already been preparing in my heart. And so, here we are—sharing stories from my walk with God, stories that reflect the forming of the Potter's hand upon the clay, and the writing of His story upon my life.

This sense of divine orchestration in sharing spiritual experiences has deep roots in Christian tradition. Julian of Norwich, despite her initial hesitations, felt compelled to share her "showings" (revelations), writing: "But God forbid that you should say or take it that I am a teacher, for that is not my meaning... I am a woman, ignorant, weak, and frail. But I know well that what I am saying I have received by the revelation of him who is a sovereign teacher" (*Revelations of Divine Love*, 14th century, Chapter 6).

GROWING UP IN FAITH

My name is Chantal Rousselle. I am a French Acadian from New Brunswick on the East Coast of Canada. I grew up in a family of seven kids in a small village near the ocean. My childhood was filled with simple joys—playing in the woods, fields, and on the shore.

We were raised in the Catholic faith, learning repetitive prayers and the act of confession. Yet, beneath the rituals and religious obligations, I always sensed a deeper spiritual presence was real, but I couldn't fully grasp it—especially when all I saw were images of Jesus dead on the cross in churches.

As far back as I can remember, I had vivid dreams. Sometimes, I'd even sleepwalk, and my mom would guide me back to bed. These dreams haunted me at times. I often found myself stepping out of my body and having adventures, whether around the house, outside, or with friends. In those moments, I felt immense freedom, as if I were tapping into something beyond the physical world. It made me realize that we are so much more than what we see.

These early spiritual experiences resonate with what Hildegard of Bingen described when she wrote about receiving visions from early childhood: "From my earliest childhood, before my bones, nerves, and veins were fully strengthened, I have always seen this vision in my soul... The light which I see is not bound by space. It is far, far brighter than a cloud which carries the sun" (*Scivias*, 12th century, Book III, Vision 10.26).

Even amidst difficulties, I could feel a presence over me, a joy that I now recognize as the Spirit of God. As a child, I would sing spontaneous songs, look up at the sky, and talk to God. It felt so natural, so intimate. I remember walking through fields, lying on the grass, and speaking to Him. At night, I would close my window and sing Him goodnight. God was very real to me.

"God has set eternity in the human heart." —Ecclesiastes 3:11 (NIV)

Even as a child, I felt eternity stirring inside me. I wasn't learning to connect with God—I was awakening to a connection that had already existed, to an eternal reality written in my very design.

A DARK TURN AND A SPIRITUAL AWAKENING

As I grew older and entered my teenage years, my life took a darker turn. I drifted away from that innocent connection with God and found myself entangled in drugs, alcohol, and brokenness. At that point, I lost sight of His presence.

Yet, even in my early twenties, before I fully gave my life to Christ, I had a pivotal dream that shook me. In the dream, I was standing in space among the stars, facing a huge closed door. I felt utterly mortified because I wasn't allowed to pass through it. On the other side was light, but I was stuck in the darkness. When I woke up, I had a clear revelation—I wasn't saved. I wasn't registered in Heaven.

Later, I had another dream where I was standing in Heaven among the stars, but there were huge gates in front of me, closed. I felt alone and on the wrong side. I woke up terrified, realizing I didn't know The Way yet.

This experience of spiritual awakening through dreams has deep precedent in Christian mystical tradition. John of the Ladder (also known as John Climacus) wrote in the 7th century: "Sleep is a particular state of nature, an image of death, an inactivity of the senses. Sleep is one, but, like desire, its sources and occasions are many: that is to say, it comes from nature, from food, from demons, and perhaps also from extreme, prolonged fasting... but God often sends dreams to us as life-giving messages" (*The Ladder of Divine Ascent*, Step 19.1).

Shortly after, something inside me began to change. My sister had given her life to Jesus and was constantly talking about Him to everyone. At first, I pushed back, even telling people not to listen to her. But then something mysterious happened. One morning, I woke up, and it felt as if the veil had been torn. Everything became clear. I knew I had to say yes to Jesus—He was The Way.

I now understand this wasn't about Jesus becoming available to me for the first time—it was about my eyes being opened to see Him clearly. The veil wasn't between Heaven and earth; it was over my perception. In that moment of awakening, I didn't create a new connection with God—I recognized the connection that had always existed.

This sudden illumination reflects what Maximus the Confessor described as "natural contemplation"—when the eyes of our understanding are opened to see spiritual realities that were always present but previously hidden from our perception (*Centuries on Love*, 7th century, First Century, 100).

DISCOVERING THE PRESENCE OF GOD

I had no idea how to live this new life, but I soon began to feel His presence so strongly. At times, I would feel myself melting into my bed or experience the atmosphere shifting at work. I could even see the substance of His presence surrounding me. It was like a divine intoxication—a secret life I was building with Him, the Lover of my soul.

I was falling deeper into a relationship with God, and the spiritual experiences I had as a child began to make sense in the light of my newfound faith. What I once thought were just strange dreams were actually early invitations to experience the heavenly realms.

This experience of divine intoxication has been beautifully expressed by mystics throughout the ages. Bernard of Clairvaux spoke of being "intoxicated with the abundance of God's house" (*Sermons on the Song of Songs*, 12th century, Sermon 7.2), while Pseudo-Dionysius described divine ecstasy as being "transported outside of oneself into the object of one's love" (*The Divine Names*, 5th century, Chapter 4.13).

A NEW ERA: THE VISION THAT CHANGED EVERYTHING

Back in 2009, I had a dream that forever changed me. It wasn't just a typical dream—it was so vivid, so real, that I knew deep down it was a divine encounter.

In this dream, I was standing in the cosmos, surrounded by stars, looking down at the earth. But the earth wasn't whole; it was broken up into pieces, floating in space. The sight was strange, but what shocked me even more was how natural it felt. I wasn't afraid; instead, I was in awe.

It felt as though I was meant to see things from this perspective, as if I were looking at reality through God's eyes.

Suddenly, the scene changed. I found myself walking on one of these floating pieces of earth, and I wasn't alone. There was a long stream of people with me, all heading toward a mountain in the distance. I had this deep, inner knowing that we were going up this mountain because the Lord was waiting for us to come up and meet Him. We were going up to see the King!

When I woke up, I knew this was no ordinary dream. It was an invitation from God, calling me up to a higher place, both spiritually and literally. I kept thinking, I've read this somewhere in the Bible, and after searching, I found it—Isaiah:

"In the last days, the mountain of Yahweh's temple will be raised up as the head of the mountains... and we will go up to the mountain of the Lord." —Isaiah 2:2 (TPT)

I couldn't believe it. I had never really known this scripture before, but there it was, perfectly describing the vision I had in my dream.

This experience mirrors what Ignatius of Loyola called "spiritual consolation"—when God speaks directly to the soul through images, Scripture, and divine insight that transcends our normal understanding. Ignatius taught that such moments of clarity and spiritual confirmation are signs of God's active presence and guidance (*Spiritual Exercises*, 16th century, Rules for Discernment, Third Rule).

At first, I wasn't sure how to talk about it. When I shared my dream with the people around me, no one seemed to really get it. It felt too big, too wild. So, I kept it close to my heart and asked the Holy Spirit to help me understand it.

I began paying closer attention to what God was revealing, and the more I focused on it, the more these types of encounters began to multiply. I knew God was leading me into a journey of exploring heavenly things—things above.

That's when Colossians 3:1-2 came alive to me:

"Christ's resurrection is your resurrection too. This is why we are to yearn for all that is above, for that's where Christ sits enthroned at the place of all power, honor, and authority!" —Colossians 3:1—2 (TPT)

This verse wasn't just an encouragement—it was an invitation to ascension. It was God telling me that I was meant to set my affection on things above, to dwell in heavenly realities, not just earthly ones. This wasn't about earning a higher spiritual status—it was about awakening to where I was already positioned in Christ.

⸪ ASCENSION ACTIVATION: SEEING FROM ABOVE ⸪

Take a moment to sit quietly with God. Ask Him to open your eyes to see from His perspective. Imagine yourself standing with Him, looking down at your current situation from a heavenly viewpoint. What changes when you see through His eyes? How does this shift in perspective change your approach to your circumstances?

THE REALITY OF HEAVENLY CITIZENSHIP

By Contrast, We Have Already Come Near to God

"By contrast, we have already come near to God in a totally different realm, the Zion-realm, for we have entered the city of the Living God, which is the New Jerusalem in Heaven! We have joined the festal gathering of myriads of angels in their joyous celebration!" —Hebrews 12:22 (TPT)

The phrase "already come" is significant. In the original Greek, the verb is in the perfect tense, meaning the fullness of our salvation and our entrance into God's heavenly realm has already been accomplished. This echoes what Paul teaches in Romans 8:29, Ephesians 2:6 (NKJV), and Colossians 3:1-4 (NKJV). Through Jesus, we have already been raised to sit with Him in heavenly places.

I deliberately return to Athanasius's bold declaration that "God became man so that man might become god" (*On the Incarnation*, 4th century, 54) because it so perfectly captures our understanding of heavenly citizenship. For Athanasius and many early Church leaders, the Incarnation wasn't simply God coming down to us—it was about raising humanity up into God's own life.

In Ephesians 3:10, we read that God's wisdom is now displayed through His people to principalities and powers in heavenly realms. It's awe-inspiring to consider why God chooses to reveal His wisdom through us! He even goes on to say in Ephesians 1:23 that He is filled by us, His Church, and we are filled by Him.

We are brought together in Him as one. His desire is that we move as He moves and speak as He speaks, partnering with Him in bringing everything back to its original intent—back to innocence.

This revelation transformed everything for me. I used to pray from a place of separation, striving to believe. Now, I pray from a place of union with Christ, and everything flows from this place. I cultivate an awareness of my oneness with Him.

For instance, not long ago, I had a dream where I stood in a waterfall that seemed to flow from Heaven. As I pressed my face into the waterfall, my voice began to sound like the Father's voice. We were one voice, speaking together, and I was receiving His desires as my own. In this dream, I saw myself translating heavenly things and bringing them into the earth. Our inclusion in Christ enables us to co-labor with Him in the restoration of all things. Everything is accessed through faith and union. It's a simple truth that challenges the religious mindset!

This experience reflects what Maximus the Confessor described as "theosis"—the transformation of the believer through participation in divine life. For Maximus, this wasn't just a future hope but a present reality that could be experienced through communion with God (*Ambigua*, 7th century, 7.22).

"And He alone is the leader and source of everything needed in the church. God has put everything beneath the authority of Jesus Christ and has given Him the highest rank above all others. And now we, His church, are His Body on the earth, and that which fills Him who is being filled by it!" —Ephesians 1:22-23 (TPT)

"The kingdom is not discovered in one place or another, for God's kingdom realm is already expanding within some of you." —Luke 17:20-21 (TPT)

THE JOY OF THE LORD

"Joy is the serious business of Heaven." —C.S. Lewis (*Letters to Malcolm: Chiefly on Prayer*, 1964, p. 93)

The Lord once gave me a funny picture: He told me He was like a marshmallow, tucking me inside of Himself. Heaven is filled with joy, and sometimes it's like a comedy. He also said I needed to "hug Him on the inside," inviting me into deeper communion within. Each time I sense separation, I picture that image, reminding myself of the truth: I am in Him.

This playful, joyful experience of God has deep roots in Christian tradition. Francis of Assisi was known for his exuberant joy, even referring to himself as "God's fool" (*Little Flowers of St. Francis*, 13th century, Chapter 8). Pseudo-Macarius wrote in the 4th century that the soul united with God "becomes all light, all face, all eye... it is filled with the spiritual fire and becomes all eye... full of the divine vision" (*Spiritual Homilies*, Homily 1.2). This vision of unity encompasses divine joy.

When you live from this perspective of oneness, fear dissolves. You become an explorer, adventuring with the Lord. Jesus taught that unless we become like children, we cannot even enter the kingdom of heaven (see Matthew 18:3).

Most of my joyful encounters with the Lord have been in the spirit— whether during sleep or while meditating on the Word. I've found myself transported to other countries, ministering the gospel, healing the sick, and serving those in need. I didn't realize that being "in the Spirit" meant being fully in Him, moving effortlessly as He moves.

When we are in the Spirit, we don't lean on our own understanding. We operate in innocence, boldness, righteousness, joy, and peace. Once, while tossing and turning in bed, I suddenly began praying in tongues over my husband in a language I had never heard. I was loud, and I thought I'd wake him, but then I realized something profound: my spirit was engaged with God, even when my soul wasn't aware! I had stepped out of my body and I was in the spirit realm and I didn't feel the shift! It was completely natural!

Praying in the Spirit doesn't simply mean praying in tongues—it means functioning from the Spirit!

THE AWAKENING OF A MARKETPLACE ECCLESIA

I let Jesus use my body like a "super suit," trusting Him, my Good Shepherd, to lead me into the greater works He promised. Because I said "yes" to the Lord and allowed Him to lead me, I now find myself flourishing alongside a team in the marketplace. Together, we cultivate ascension, seeking divine intelligence, wisdom, and discernment from God.

"But those who live by the impulses of the Holy Spirit are motivated to pursue spiritual realities." —Romans 8:5 (TPT)

We are called to manifest the immeasurable power of the unseen realm in the physical world. Christ in us—the hope of glory! (Colossians 1:27)

This integration of spiritual reality in the marketplace reflects what Brother Lawrence practiced as "the presence of God" in everyday tasks. For Lawrence, there was no division between sacred and secular—every moment and every task could be infused with divine awareness and communion (The *Practice of the Presence of God*, 17th century, Third Conversation).

A JOURNEY OF DISCOVERY: BRYAN'S RESPONSE

As an engineer grounded in logic and reason, I'm probably the least likely person to be writing a book about spiritual realms and the limitless expanse of Heaven. But by the grace of God, here I am! Let that be a testimony to those who feel unsuited or ill-equipped to read the words we've written.

Throughout my journey, I've come to realize that God has designed a unique way for each of us to connect with Him. For me, it's been a gradual awakening, like exercising a muscle. With every step into the spiritual, I've learned to shift my consciousness, and with each shift, I've experienced new dimensions of His presence.

Though the journey has its ups and downs, one thing has become clear: when God opens a door and invites us into a deeper spiritual realm, He makes that realm available to us permanently. The more we exercise and engage with it, the more expansive it becomes.

This progressive spiritual growth resembles what Gregory of Nyssa called "epektasis"—the soul's eternal progress into the infinite depths of God. For Gregory, spiritual growth wasn't a linear path to a fixed destination but an eternal journey of discovery, where each new revelation of God's glory leads to ever-greater heights of wonder and communion (*Life of Moses*, 4th century, Book II.239).

This book is designed to progressively deepen your understanding and experience of ascension—guiding you practically into the profound realms of faith and spiritual realities available to every believer. Take your time with each chapter. Engage deeply with the scriptures and reflection questions provided, and consider journaling your insights or discussing them in community with others. Our prayer is that this journey will awaken you to a greater measure of God's Kingdom here and now, preparing you for the fullness of His glory—not simply a future hope, but a reality already unfolding and continually being unveiled within you.

"Things never discovered or heard of before, things beyond our ability to imagine—these are the many things God has in store for all His lovers." —1 Corinthians 2:9 (TPT)

Let's journey together into the deeper realms of what God has in store, embracing the "now" while eagerly anticipating the "not yet."

THE MOUNTAIN OF THE LORD: A DIVINE INVITATION

"In the last days, the mountain of Yahweh's temple will be raised up as the head of the mountains, towering over all the hills. A sparkling stream of every nation will flow into it. Many peoples will come and say, 'Everyone, come! Let's go up higher to Yahweh's mountain, to the house of Jacob's God; then He can teach us His ways and we can walk in His paths!' Zion will be the center of instruction, and the word of Yahweh will go out from Jerusalem." —Isaiah 2:2-3 (TPT)

Isaiah stood at the threshold of a mystical encounter, his senses caught between the earthly and the divine. He saw a vision unfold before him—

heaven and earth converging, reality bending as the mountain of Yahweh rose above all others, towering in supreme majesty.

This vision parallels what Dionysius the Areopagite described as "mystical ascent"—the soul's journey upward through progressive illumination toward union with God. For Dionysius, this ascent involved moving beyond conceptual knowledge into direct experience of divine reality (*Mystical Theology*, 5th century, Chapter 1.1).

This was no ordinary peak; it radiated the very light of creation, a beacon of divine presence that drew the nations upward like a magnetic force. Streams of people from every land moved against the laws of nature, ascending toward the throne of God as if compelled by an unseen power. It was a supernatural movement—rivers flowing uphill toward the heart of God (Isaiah 2:2, TPT).

The air shimmered with anticipation. The nations cried out in unity, "Everyone, come! Let's go up higher!" (Isaiah 2:3). Their voices carried an urgency, a deep hunger to know the ways of Yahweh. This was not just a pilgrimage—it was an awakening, a call to step into a higher realm of revelation and transformation.

Each step toward Zion was not merely physical; it was a soul-deep ascent into the wisdom of God. The people weren't just going up a mountain—they were being drawn into the very presence of Yahweh Himself.

At the heart of this vision stands Jesus—the true desire of the nations (Haggai 2:7). He is the fulfillment of every longing heart, the ultimate expression of God's love and wisdom. As the nations ascend, it is Jesus they encounter. He is the one drawing humanity to Himself, inviting every tribe and tongue into His presence. In Him, the deepest desires of every heart find their fulfillment. He is the convergence point, the radiant pinnacle, the One whose glory compels nations upward. In Jesus, the nations do not merely find instruction—they discover the very essence of life, love, and divine purpose.

THE LAW OF DIVINE MAGNETISM: GOD IS ALWAYS DRAWING US HIGHER

What Isaiah witnessed defied logic—rivers flowing upward, people being drawn by an unseen force. Just as gravity pulls water downward, something far greater was at work here—the divine pull of God's presence.

The Spirit of Yahweh was reversing the natural order, restoring everything that was broken, reclaiming everything lost. This is the nature of ascension—God drawing us higher, lifting us out of earthly constraints, expanding our vision, and calling us to live from His perspective.

This divine magnetism reflects what Bernard of Clairvaux described as "the soul's journey to God"—a movement propelled not by human effort but by divine love. Bernard taught that it is God's love that draws us upward, and our response is simply to yield to this pull (On Loving God, 12th century, Chapter 7).

The closer the people came to Zion, the more they were transformed—awakened. Their hunger deepened, their understanding sharpened. The light of Yahweh dispelled the shadows of falsehood, and as they ascended, they stepped into a greater awareness of divine reality. They weren't just learning about God—they were being reshaped by the very encounter.

This is ascension. This is what it means to rise into the fullness of God's Kingdom.

THE DIVINE FREQUENCY: ALIGNING WITH HEAVEN'S REALITY

Before we explore this section together, I want to invite you into a perspective that bridges ancient biblical truth with how we understand creation today. Throughout Scripture, we see that God's presence has tangible effects on the physical world—from the burning bush that wasn't consumed to the fire that fell on Elijah's altar. The Bible often describes God's presence using physical properties like light, fire, and glory. What I share here is simply an exploration of how God's unchanging nature interfaces with His creation, using language that helps us grasp spiritual realities through analogies we can understand.

Allow me to geek out for a moment as an engineer...

When one of my engineering professors first explained resonant frequency to me, he used a hilarious example of an opera singer shattering a wine glass with her voice. "That glass didn't break because the singer was off-key," he quipped, "it broke because she was perfectly in tune with the glass's natural frequency." Little did I know that this principle would one day help me understand the mechanics of Heaven touching Earth!

Let me explain what actually happens when that glass shatters. Every physical object in our world has what scientists call a natural frequency—a rate at which it naturally wants to vibrate when disturbed. This isn't mystical mumbo-jumbo; it's fundamental physics. When you tap a wine glass gently with a spoon, it rings at a specific pitch. That's its natural frequency, determined by its physical properties like mass, shape, and the material it's made from.

Here's where it gets fascinating: When an opera singer produces a note that exactly matches the natural frequency of the glass, something remarkable happens. Each sound wave that hits the glass adds a tiny bit of energy to it, causing it to vibrate slightly. Normally, these vibrations would dissipate. But when the frequency perfectly matches, each new wave arrives at precisely the right moment to amplify the previous vibration, creating what engineers call "constructive interference."

It's like pushing a child on a swing. If you push at random times, the swing moves erratically. But if you push at exactly the right moment in each swing cycle (matching its natural frequency), even small pushes accumulate into powerful motion. The glass vibrates more and more intensely until the molecular bonds in the material can no longer hold together—and it shatters.

This is pure science, not new age philosophy. It's the same principle that engineers must account for when designing bridges (to prevent collapse during resonant winds), buildings (to withstand earthquakes), and even everyday machines like washing machines (which use counterweights to prevent excessive vibration during the spin cycle).

The remarkable thing is that frequencies aren't limited to sound waves—they're foundational to all of reality. Light, radio, electricity, atomic particles—everything in our universe operates according to frequency principles. Even our brainwaves can be measured in different frequency bands (delta, theta, alpha, beta, gamma), each corresponding to different states of consciousness.

When I talk about Heaven's frequency, I'm not introducing some mystical concept divorced from physical reality. I'm suggesting that the biblical concept of Heaven and Earth isn't about two disconnected places but two different vibrational states of the same reality—one that we can experience by aligning our spiritual "frequency" with God's presence, just as precisely as that opera singer aligns her voice with the glass.

This isn't new age thinking—it's ancient biblical wisdom understood through the lens of modern physics. When Scripture speaks of God's voice creating reality, of Jesus speaking and nature responding, of setting our minds on things above, it's describing a frequency-based reality where alignment with higher spiritual frequencies literally transforms physical circumstances.

THE QUANTUM BLUEPRINT: GOD'S MASTERFUL DESIGN

What modern science now glimpses through quantum physics, God has known from the beginning. The quantum realm—where particles can exist in multiple places simultaneously, where observation affects reality, and where interconnectedness defies our classical understanding of separation—reveals a universe far more aligned with spiritual truth than we previously recognized.

The most astonishing revelation of quantum physics may be just how "empty" physical reality truly is. If we could remove all the empty space in atoms, the entire human race—all 8 billion people—would fit into a volume just slightly larger than a golf ball while maintaining their collective mass. That's because atoms are approximately 99.9999999999996% empty space. What we perceive as solid matter is actually mostly nothing! When you "touch" any object, you're not making actual contact with it; rather, you're experiencing the electromagnetic repulsion between the electron fields of your atoms and those of the object. No physical object ever truly "touches" another at the quantum level.

This scientific reality forces us to question our most basic assumptions about physical existence. The desk beneath your hands, the floor beneath your feet, even your own body—these seemingly solid objects are mostly empty space, held together by invisible forces and fields of energy. What appears most "real" to our senses is largely an illusion, while the invisible forces that actually govern reality remain hidden from view.

In the quantum world, solid matter dissolves into probability waves and energy patterns. The chair you're sitting on, seemingly solid and unchangeable, is actually a vibrating collection of subatomic particles held together by invisible forces. This scientific reality beautifully affirms what Scripture has always declared: "By faith we understand that the universe was formed at God's command, so that what is seen was not made out of what was visible" (Hebrews 11:3, NIV).

God has masterfully woven the seen and unseen realms together, creating a reality where the material world emerges from and responds to the immaterial. The very existence of quantum entanglement—where particles separated by vast distances instantly affect one another—points to a universe where everything is fundamentally connected in ways that transcend time and space. This reflects the spiritual truth that in Christ, "all things hold together" (Colossians 1:17, NIV).

Perhaps most mind-boggling is the famous double-slit experiment, which has been replicated countless times to the continued amazement of scientists. In this experiment, photons or electrons are fired at a barrier with two slits, creating an interference pattern on a screen behind it—as if the particles are behaving like waves passing through both slits simultaneously. But remarkably, when scientists observe which slit the particles pass through, the interference pattern disappears, and the particles behave like solid objects going through just one slit. The mere act of observation changes how matter behaves at the fundamental level.

This experiment reveals a profound truth: consciousness affects physical reality. The observer isn't separate from what is being observed—they're intimately connected. How beautifully this aligns with spiritual principles! Just as our attention and intention can influence quantum behavior, our faith and spiritual awareness can transform the reality around us. When Scripture speaks of being "transformed by the renewing of your mind" (Romans 12:2), perhaps it's pointing to this very power—our consciousness, aligned with Christ's, has the capacity to participate in the manifestation of Kingdom realities into our physical world.

[Quantum Entanglement Side Note] For the quantum physics enthusiasts: Entanglement is perhaps one of the most mind-bending aspects of quantum mechanics. Einstein famously called it "spooky action at a distance." When two particles become entangled, they essentially become one system, and what happens to one instantly affects the other—regardless of whether they're separated by inches or light-years. This defies our classical understanding of locality and separateness. I can't help but see this as God's way of building connectivity into the very fabric of creation—a scientific testimony to the spiritual reality that in Christ, we are "all members of one body" (Ephesians 4:25). When Paul wrote about being "seated with Christ in heavenly places" while still physically on earth, perhaps he was describing a spiritual entanglement far more real than we've understood!

METANOIA: THE AWAKENED MIND

The Greek understanding of mind transformation goes far deeper than our modern concept of simply changing our thinking patterns. What Scripture calls "the renewing of your mind" (Romans 12:2) was expressed in the original language as "metanoia" —a concept that revolutionizes how we understand faith itself:

"The word μετάνοια metanoia... does not mean repentance! It suggests an awakening to the awareness of God's thoughts; from meta, together with and noieō, to perceive with the mind. It describes the awakening of the mind to that which is true; a re-alignment of one's reasoning; it is a gathering of one's thoughts, a co-knowing. Faith is not a decision; it is a discovery... Metanoia means to discover God's thoughts about us; literally, to co-know... The metanoia moment awakens in us an inevitable return to our redeemed, authentic Genesis."—Francois du Toit, *Mirror Study Bible*

This profound understanding of metanoia perfectly aligns with ascension consciousness. Metanoia is a complete transformation of our thinking to align with God's perspective. We're not attempting to create new thoughts or force ourselves to believe certain concepts. Rather, we're awakening to what has always been true —our thoughts aligning with Heaven's frequency as we become aware of our seated position with Christ. In this light, faith isn't something we muster up through mental effort; it's what naturally emerges as our perception shifts from earthly limitations to heavenly realities.

The quantum aspects of consciousness and the biblical concept of metanoia converge to reveal a powerful truth: transformation occurs not through striving but through awakening. As our mind aligns with our spirit's reality, we naturally begin to vibrate at Heaven's frequency, enabling us to experience and release the Kingdom in entirely new dimensions.

SACRED AND SECULAR UNITED: THE GREAT CONVERGENCE

Through Christ's incarnation and resurrection, every false boundary between Heaven and earth, the sacred and the secular, the mystical and the theological, the supernatural and the natural has been erased forever.

What humanity once perceived as separation was never real—only a veil of misunderstanding. The veil has been torn.

Now, in Christ, the fullness of God's presence is revealed in all things, inviting us to live in the seamless reality of His Kingdom, here and now!

The incarnation wasn't merely God visiting His creation—it was divinity permanently weaving itself into the fabric of humanity. When the eternal Word became flesh and "made his dwelling among us" (John 1:14, NIV), He forever sanctified physical existence. The material world wasn't something to escape but something to transform through divine presence.

Then in the resurrection, Jesus didn't simply revive—He revealed an entirely new mode of existence where spiritual and natural realities were perfectly integrated. His resurrected body could eat fish on the shore and yet pass through locked doors. He could be touched by Thomas yet ascend to the Father. This wasn't a contradiction but a demonstration of creation's true design—natural and supernatural united as one.

Ascension is an Invitation to Action.

"He will teach us His ways, and we will walk in His paths." —Isaiah 2:3 (TPT)

Ascension is not just an experience—it is a mandate, a divine invitation to understand God's ways and embody them on the earth. The higher we climb, the more Heaven entrusts us with its wisdom and authority. Yet, this ascension is not the result of striving or toil; it is the effortless outcome of opening our hearts wider to God's grace. We don't ascend by human strength—we simply yield and allow ourselves to fall forward into the arms of our loving Father. In His embrace, we are lifted higher, transformed by His presence, recalibrated to the frequency of Heaven so we can release its reality into the world.

As Gyene Gagnon beautifully says, "We ascend as vapor, drawn upward by the warmth of His love, effortlessly rising into union with Him."

As Maximus the Confessor taught, "The purpose of spiritual ascent is not escape from the world but the transformation of the world" (*Centuries on Love*, 7th century, Third Century, 25). For Maximus, heavenly contemplation always led to earthly action—bringing divine reality into human experience. This seamless integration of heavenly encounters with earthly purpose reveals the true nature of ascension.

Gregory of Nyssa expressed this divine continuity when he wrote, "The spiritual journey is a continuous progression into the infinite" (*Life of Moses*, 4th century, Book II.239). There is no separation between our ascent and our transformative presence on earth—they form a continuous, unbroken reality in Christ.

Everything in creation vibrates at a specific frequency. From physical matter to thoughts and emotions, all reality operates on vibrational patterns. Heaven itself resonates at the highest frequency—pure love, joy, and divine harmony. When we understand this principle, ascension becomes the process of aligning our spiritual frequency with Heaven's resonance.

What if...

? What if our greatest limitation is not where we are, but what we believe about where we are?

? What if God is always calling us higher, yet we hesitate because we think we are unworthy, unready, or unable?

? What if the only thing stopping us from stepping into greater realities is our own reluctance to leave behind what is familiar?

The call to ascend demands surrender. A willingness to let go of lesser things to step into greater glory. The mountain of Yahweh is not a place we visit—it is a realm we are called to dwell in.

HEAVEN'S FREQUENCY: LIVING IN DIVINE ALIGNMENT

At Flō, we've discovered that approaching spiritual reality through the lens of frequency has transformed how we operate in both spiritual and natural realms. As we attune ourselves to Heaven's frequency through childlike faith, thanksgiving, humor, celebration, and honor, we create an atmosphere where divine possibilities become manifest realities.

Jesus demonstrated this principle perfectly after His resurrection. When He appeared to His disciples in a locked room (John 20:19, NKJV), He wasn't breaking natural laws—He was revealing their deeper purpose. His resurrected body showed us how creation was designed to respond to its Creator.

UNDERSTANDING HEAVEN'S REALITY

Think of it this way:

- Our ordinary physical world operates like solid building blocks—fixed and limited

- Heaven's reality flows like water—alive, dynamic, and able to move through barriers

Jesus could exist in both states at once. He could be physically touched and could eat fish with His disciples, yet He could also appear in locked rooms. This wasn't magic—it was a demonstration of creation responding perfectly to God's original design.

When Jesus moved through what appeared solid, He showed us that physical barriers aren't ultimate limits. This reveals the seamless connection between Heaven and earth that has always existed by God's design. Jesus wasn't operating against nature; He was showing nature's true potential when aligned with its Creator.

LIVING IN HEAVEN'S FREQUENCY

The implications for us are life-changing. As we align with Heaven's frequency, a transformation happens:

- Our words begin to carry creative power

- Our presence brings peace to troubled situations

- Our faith accesses possibilities that seemed impossible before

This is why Paul urges us to "set your minds on things above" (Colossians 3:2). He knew that where we focus our attention shapes our entire reality.

As Simone Weil observed, "Attention is the rarest and purest form of generosity." When we give our full attention to heavenly realities, we open ourselves to receive and transmit God's presence with remarkable clarity.

Just as God spoke creation into existence from His realm of unlimited potential, we too can participate in bringing Heaven's possibilities into earthly reality. When we ascend in our awareness to heavenly places, we align with God's creative design and become conduits for His Kingdom to manifest here and now.

In our Flō community, we've noticed that as we intentionally cultivate an atmosphere of childlike wonder, celebration, generosity, and honor, the frequency of our environment shifts. Problems that seemed insurmountable at lower frequencies often dissolve when approached from Heaven's higher vibration. Solutions emerge that weren't visible before. Creativity flows. Relationships heal. Resources multiply.

Remarkably, modern science confirms what Scripture has always taught about thanksgiving. When we give thanks, our bodies release oxytocin and other beneficial hormones that reduce stress and promote healing. Research has even shown that grateful people emit different patterns of photons—light particles—than those experiencing negative emotions.

This isn't metaphorical—it's measurable. The frequency of fear vibrates at approximately 100 Hz, while love vibrates at 528 Hz. As we choose love over fear, our entire being recalibrates to a frequency more aligned with Heaven's reality. This is why worship, gratitude, and joy are such powerful spiritual technologies—they literally raise our frequency to match Heaven's resonance.

When Jesus taught us to pray "on earth as it is in heaven," He was instructing us in the art of frequency matching. Heaven already operates in perfect harmony, abundance, health, and peace. Our role is not to create these realities but to align with their frequency so they can manifest through us into the physical world.

The beautiful paradox is that this high-frequency living isn't achieved through intense spiritual striving—quite the opposite. It emerges naturally as we embrace childlike simplicity, rest in God's presence, and allow our hearts to be tuned by the Master Musician. Like instruments in an orchestra, we each play our unique part while following the Conductor's direction. We don't create the music through effort; we contribute to the symphony by faithfully playing the specific notes we've been given, creating harmony as we stay attuned to His timing and direction.

At Flō, we're learning to live in this heavenly frequency together—celebrating small victories, honoring each person's unique contribution, approaching challenges with holy humor, and feasting on God's goodness even before we see the manifestation. The result has been a corporate elevation in both spiritual experience and practical outcomes that would have been impossible at lower frequencies of doubt, striving, or fear.

Your invitation into ascension is simultaneously an invitation into frequency alignment. As you yield to the Father's embrace, you'll find your entire being naturally beginning to vibrate in harmony with Heaven's song—and what you release from that position will carry the unmistakable resonance of eternity.

PRACTICAL APPLICATION: FIRST STEPS OF ASCENSION

As we close this first chapter, we invite you to take your first steps into the practice of ascension with this simple exercise—one that helps you begin to attune to Heaven's frequency and experience the seamless reality of God's presence:

1 *Create Sacred Space:* Find a quiet place where you won't be disturbed for 10-15 minutes. Remember that in quantum reality, your intention literally creates a field of potential—you're not just choosing a location but establishing a resonant environment.

2 *Center Your Being:* Close your eyes and take several deep breaths, releasing any tension or distractions. With each inhale, imagine drawing in the higher frequency of God's presence; with each exhale, release lower frequencies of fear, doubt, or distraction.

3 *Shift Frequency:* Begin to shift your awareness from your natural surroundings to the presence of God within and around you. This isn't about going somewhere else but recognizing the quantum reality that divine presence already permeates everything.

4 *Divine Entanglement:* Picture yourself being enveloped in God's presence—like being tucked inside a marshmallow, as Chantal described. Just as quantum particles remain connected across distance, recognize your eternal connection with God that transcends all separation.

5 *Permission Prayer:* Say these words: "Lord, I give you permission to take me wherever You want to go. I surrender to Your leading. I align my frequency with Yours."

6 *Receptive Rest:* Don't strive or try to make anything happen. Simply rest and receive. Remember that ascension isn't about effort but alignment—like a radio tuning to a broadcast that's already transmitting.

7 *Divine Download:* Pay attention to any impressions, sensations, or images that come to mind. These are like data packets from Heaven's realm being downloaded into your consciousness.

8 *Record Reality:* After your time of quiet, journal what you experienced, even if it seems small or insignificant. This act of recording helps integrate higher-frequency experiences into your everyday awareness.

This practice resembles what Teresa of Ávila called "the prayer of recollection"—a simple exercise of turning inward to recognize God's presence within, which she taught was the gateway to deeper spiritual experience (*The Way of Perfection*, 16th century, Chapter 28). In modern terms, we might call it a "frequency recalibration"—aligning your entire being with the higher vibrations of Heaven's reality.

As physicist and theologian John Polkinghorne notes, "Prayer is quantum entanglement at the spiritual level—a non-local connection that transcends the limitations of space and time" (*Science and Christian Belief*, 1994, p. 83). When you enter this state of prayerful receptivity, you're participating in the quantum nature of spiritual reality.

Remember, ascension is not about achieving a spiritual experience through your own effort—it's about awakening to a reality that already exists because of your union with Christ. The veil between Heaven and Earth isn't something you need to penetrate—it's an illusion already dissolved through Christ's finished work. Start where you are, with childlike faith, and allow God to guide you into deeper dimensions of His presence.

In the next chapter, we'll explore more fully what ascension is and how it transforms our daily lives as believers.

CHAPTER 2: 🔥 WHAT IS ASCENSION?

Side effects may include: ✅ Spontaneously seeing heavenly realities in ordinary moments ✅ Finding yourself engaging with God more naturally than ever before ✅ No longer striving for what you realize you already have

THE INVITATION TO LIVE FROM YOUR TRUE POSITION

Ascension is not an abstract concept—it is the invitation to live from our true position in Christ. It is not an escape from this world, nor is it reserved for the super-spiritual. It is our normal state of being in Him.

We were never meant to struggle through life from a place of limitation. We were designed to function from the heavenly realms, where our spirits are already co-seated with Christ (Ephesians 2:6, NKJV).

This understanding of our heavenly position has deep roots in Christian tradition. As Origen of Alexandria wrote in the 3rd century, "The spirit of man is the lamp of the Lord... Within each of us is a divine light, a participation in the very nature of God Himself" (*On First Principles*, Book I, ch. 3.5). This participation in divine nature—what the Eastern church calls *theosis*—is at the heart of ascension.

What if Heaven isn't somewhere far away, but fully accessible right now? What if your spirit already knows how to engage with the realms of God, but your mind just hasn't caught up yet?

This concept of experiencing Heaven while still on earth might sound unusual to some readers, but it's deeply rooted in Scripture. When Paul writes that God has "raised us up with Christ and seated us with him in the heavenly realms" (Ephesians 2:6), he uses the past tense—indicating this is already our position in Christ. Throughout church history, devoted believers like Brother Lawrence, who practiced "the presence of God" in everyday tasks, and Teresa of Ávila, who described the "interior castle" of communion with God, have embraced this reality. Their testimonies and writings reveal that intimate experience of God's presence isn't just for eternity—it's the inheritance of every believer right now.

For most of my life, I didn't understand this. I approached faith with logic and reason, seeing only what was in front of me. The idea of experiencing Heaven in real-time was completely foreign to me. But when I encountered the Holy Spirit in a way I couldn't deny, everything changed.

I realized that Heaven is not a future destination—it is a present reality that we are called to engage with now.

LIVING FROM ABOVE—THE MOMENT EVERYTHING SHIFTED

"Set your minds on things above, not on earthly things." —Colossians 3:2 (NIV)

Throughout Scripture, we see God working through ordinary moments to reveal extraordinary truths. Moses encountered God in a burning bush while tending sheep. David received his kingly anointing while caring for his father's flock. Peter received his revelation about the Gentiles while on a rooftop waiting for lunch. What I'm about to share is my own "ordinary moment" that became sacred ground—not because I was seeking a profound experience, but because God is faithful to reveal Himself to those who sincerely seek Him.

I share this not as someone who has "arrived" spiritually, but as a fellow traveler who stumbled upon something beautiful that I believe is available to every believer through the finished work of Christ.

I'll never forget the first time I truly experienced ascension.

It happened during a prayer gathering at Flō. I wasn't striving or trying to have some extraordinary experience—I simply turned my heart toward Jesus, becoming still, resting in His presence. It's a simple shift of consciousness into the heavenly realms.

And then, something shifted.

Suddenly, I felt a remarkable sense of lightness, as if my spirit was gently being drawn upward. Initially, it was subtle—like stepping into a new atmosphere filled with profound peace. Then, the sensation became clearer, as though my spirit was rising, while my body remained perfectly still. With childlike wonder, I allowed my imagination to run free with Jesus as we embarked on a joyful, heavenly adventure.

For a moment, I hesitated. Could this be real? Was this merely my imagination?

Yet, that moment changed everything. I realized I wasn't trying to reach Heaven; I was already there. Ascension wasn't about forging a new connection—it was about awakening to the reality of the connection I'd always had. It wasn't about earning access to a higher realm—it was about recognizing where my spirit had always been positioned, seated with Christ in heavenly places.

Before our group ascensions at Flō, I often find myself spontaneously stepping into the ascended realm—even during a casual walk to the water cooler! This beautiful mingling of Heaven and Earth has become a joyful, daily reality, continuously expanding as my awareness awakens more deeply to His presence. We live simultaneously in Heaven and on Earth, truly multidimensional beings designed to engage both realms effortlessly.

My experience echoes what Augustine described in his *Confessions*: "You were within me, but I was outside... You were with me, but I was not with you" (*Confessions*, 4th century, Book X, ch. 27). Like Augustine, I discovered that my separation from heavenly reality existed only in my perception, not in actuality.

From that day forward, ascension became a way of life.

? **Wonder Questions:**

? Have you ever had moments where you sensed a "shift" in your spirit during prayer or worship?

? What might happen if you simply became aware of your seated position with Christ, rather than trying to reach it?

CHANTAL'S STORY—DISCOVERING THE REALITY OF ASCENSION

My experiences with ascension began much earlier—before I even had words for it. As a child, I would have vivid dreams of being in other places, walking in realms of light, encountering angels, and sensing the nearness of Jesus. I didn't always understand what was happening, but I knew it was real.

My childhood experiences resemble what Hildegard of Bingen described of her own early mystical encounters: "From my earliest childhood, before my bones, nerves, and veins were fully strengthened, I have always seen this vision in my soul... The light which I see is not confined by place. It is far brighter than a cloud which carries the sun" (*Scivias*, 12th century, Book I, Vision 1).

One of my most profound encounters happened late one night.

"I was lying in bed, just praying, when suddenly, I felt myself lifting—my body was still in bed, but my spirit was moving. I had never felt anything like it. I became aware of Heaven's atmosphere surrounding me—waves of love, sounds of music, laughter. I realized, 'this is normal. This is what we were made for.'"

Since then, my experiences have deepened—visions, encounters, divine instructions in the night, prophetic insight that comes not from striving, but from resting in the reality of Heaven.

We both came from very different backgrounds, but our stories converged in this truth:

🔥 Heaven is not somewhere we go—it is where we are seated.

🔥 We were never meant to wait for access—we were born with it.

🔥 Jesus is always inviting us to "come up here" (Revelation 4:1 (NKJV)).

As Teresa of Ávila wrote centuries ago, "The soul ascending to God is like one who enters a castle made of a single diamond... wherein are many rooms, just as in Heaven there are many mansions" (*The Interior Castle*, 16th century, First Mansion, Chapter 1). Her vision of the "interior castle" reflects the same reality we're describing—ascension is the journey of awakening to the heavenly realms that have always been accessible to the believer.

WHAT EXACTLY IS ASCENSION?

Ascension is the practice of living from our seated position in Christ—accessing and experiencing heavenly realities while still on earth. It's not about leaving our bodies or escaping the physical world; it's about aligning our awareness with our true spiritual position.

Pseudo—Dionysius, writing in the 5th century, described this as "mystical theology"—the journey of the soul beyond conceptual knowledge into direct experience of divine reality. For Dionysius, this wasn't about physical displacement but spiritual elevation, where the mind transcends its normal operations to function at a higher level of awareness (*Mystical Theology*, Chapter 1.3).

In simple terms, ascension is:

- *Awakening to where we already are in Christ*
- *Shifting our consciousness from earthly to heavenly perspective*
- *Engaging with God's Kingdom as a present reality*
- *Living from Heaven to earth, not earth to Heaven*

When we ascend, we're not going somewhere new—we're becoming aware of where we already are in the Spirit. It's like adjusting the focus of a camera; the heavenly realm has always been there, but now we can see it clearly. The veil was torn once and for all at the cross, but our eyes are only now being opened to see what this means for us.

Think of it like tuning a radio to a station that's been broadcasting all along. The music doesn't start playing when you find the right frequency—it's been playing continuously. You simply align your receiver to access what has always been available.

As Maximus the Confessor wrote in the 7th century, "The whole spiritual world appears mystically imprinted on the whole sensible world... and the whole sensible world is mystically explained in the whole spiritual world" (*Ambigua*, 7.15). For Maximus, Heaven and earth were never truly separate—they were always interpenetrating realities waiting to be recognized by awakened spiritual senses.

HOW DO WE ASCEND?

Ascension is not striving to reach Heaven—it is living from our heavenly position.

Ways we engage with ascension:

Sanctified Imagination—Our imagination is a bridge between realms. When we turn it toward God, He speaks through images, impressions, and visions.

Before we explore how imagination relates to our spiritual life, it's important to understand that Scripture itself affirms the proper use of our imaginative faculty. When God told Ezekiel to 'see with your eyes, hear with your ears, and give attention to everything I am going to show you' (Ezekiel 40:4), He was engaging the prophet's sanctified imagination. The Puritans, known for their doctrinal precision and devotion to Scripture, frequently practiced what they called 'biblical meditation'—using their God-given imagination to place themselves within biblical narratives to encounter the living God. What I'm describing isn't creating mental fiction, but rather allowing the Holy Spirit to utilize a faculty God Himself designed for divine encounter.

The role of imagination in spiritual experience was well understood by Ignatius of Loyola, who developed "composition of place"—a spiritual practice where one vividly imagines oneself present in biblical scenes or heavenly realities. For Ignatius, this wasn't mere fantasy but a means of engaging spiritual reality through sanctified imagination (*Spiritual Exercises*, 16th century, Second Week).

🔥 *Stillness & Awareness*—By quieting our souls, we can sense the supernatural atmosphere of Heaven around us.

The Desert Fathers practiced what they called hesychasm—a form of prayer characterized by stillness and inner quiet. As Isaac the Syrian wrote, "Enter eagerly into the treasure house that lies within you, and so you will see the treasure house of Heaven, for the two are one and the same" (*Ascetical Homilies*, 7th century, Homily 2).

🔥 *Rhema Word*—When Scripture comes alive, it is God's direct voice to us, inviting us into deeper engagement.

🔥 *Dreams & Visions*—Many times, Heaven speaks when our natural minds are at rest.

Gregory the Great taught that "God speaks to us in sleep when our mind is at rest" (*Dialogues*, 6th century, Book IV, ch. 48). Throughout Christian history, dreams, and visions have been recognized as legitimate avenues of divine communication and heavenly encounter.

For me, ascension began as small impressions, but the more I engaged, the more vivid and real it became.

GOING WITH THE FLOW—HOW ASCENSION UNFOLDS NATURALLY

In my experiences of ascension, I've learned the importance of simply going with the flow—letting go of control or resistance. The experience can manifest in various ways:

🔥 A subtle feeling—a deep peace or awareness that you've stepped into something beyond the natural

🔥 A fleeting visual—a quick flash of light, an angel, or an image from Heaven

🔥 A song, sound, or voice—hearing something from the Spirit realm

Often, it's not a vivid vision but more of an impression, like when I saw an angel in a quick flash. There's a temptation to dismiss these impressions, but I've learned that when I speak them out loud, clarity follows, and God affirms what I'm sensing.

This receptive approach to spiritual experience mirrors what Bernard of Clairvaux called "loving attention"—a state of alert receptivity to divine movements. Bernard taught that divine revelation often begins subtly and becomes clearer as we respond in faith (*On the Song of Songs*, 12th century, Sermon 83).

Scripture implies that our spirit can perceive and interact with the spiritual realm in ways that mirror our physical senses. The Bible speaks of "tasting and seeing that the Lord is good" (Psalm 34:8), hearing the voice of God, and perceiving spiritual realities. This suggests that believers can experience the supernatural through spiritual sight, sound, and touch—we are designed to engage with Heaven.

Origen of Alexandria elaborated on this concept of spiritual senses, teaching that "there is a divine sense... blessed are those who have it. This sense takes in divine things... It sees God, hears the divine voice, smells the fragrance of Christ" (*Against Celsus*, 3rd century, Book I, 48). For Origen, these spiritual senses weren't metaphorical but real faculties that could be developed through spiritual practice.

For context, as a logical engineer in the marketplace, this shift was massive for me. I rarely dream or remember my dreams, yet I am surrounded by those who do.

We must become like children—open, curious, full of wonder, and ready to receive.

When we receive an image, we shouldn't dismiss it. Instead, we should remain in a state of rest and wonder, allowing ourselves to see where we are shown or taken next.

⁚ ASCENSION ACTIVATION: YOUR FIRST STEP ⁚

Purpose: Experience the reality of being seated with Christ

Time Needed: 5-10 minutes

Preparation:

- Find a quiet place where you won't be disturbed
- Sit comfortably and take a few deep breaths
- Let go of any expectations or pressure to "perform"

Steps:

1. Close your eyes and declare: "I am seated with Christ in heavenly places"
2. Release all striving and simply rest in God's presence
3. Ask the Holy Spirit to open the eyes of your heart
4. Notice any impressions, feelings, or images that come
5. Don't analyze or judge—simply receive with childlike faith
6. Thank God for what He shows you, even if it seems small

What You Might Experience:

- A sense of peace or lightness
- An awareness of God's presence surrounding you
- A mental image or impression
- A Scripture or word coming to mind

•   Simply a quiet knowing

Remember: You're not trying to create an experience—you're becoming aware of what's already true.

THE POWER OF CORPORATE ASCENSION

I've noticed that when we gather to ascend, these experiences increase and happen naturally.

There is something that happens when we come together in faith, in unity, with the intention to engage Heaven. The atmosphere is charged with the presence of Jesus, as He promised in Matthew 18:20.

This corporate dimension of spiritual experience was well understood in the monastic tradition. The Benedictines, for instance, recognized that communal prayer created a heightened atmosphere of divine presence. As Bernard of Clairvaux noted, "Where brethren dwell together in unity, there the Lord commands a blessing" (*Sermons on the Song of Songs*, 12th century, Sermon 23). This blessing often manifested as increased spiritual perception and divine encounter.

At times, I hear the laughter of Heaven, a voice, or even a song or sound. Sometimes I close my eyes; other times, I keep a notepad ready during ascension.

The visuals flow in different ways—sometimes as clear visions, sometimes as subtle impressions. Often, I keep my eyes open and write down what I sense. The key is to tune into our spirit's awareness, without discrediting or dismissing any part of the experience.

It's about allowing and receiving what God is revealing, which is why we enter the realm of Shalom—to become fully aware of His revelations.

FLŌ'S TRANSFORMATION: WHEN A BUSINESS BECOMES AN EKKLESIA

At Flō, ascension has become more than a practice—it has become the foundation of how we operate. What started as a simple prayer team has now evolved into a Kingdom intelligence hub, where every decision, strategy, and breakthrough is fueled by the realities of Heaven.

As we stated earlier, the integration of spiritual practice and marketplace activity reflects what the medieval Benedictines understood through their motto "ora et labora" (prayer and work). They recognized that through the practice of continual prayer, even ordinary work could become a vehicle for divine manifestation (*The Rule of St. Benedict*, 6th century, Chapter 48).

Prayer flows in many beautiful forms—from restful silence and extended listening, to ascension prayer, or simply holding others lovingly in our hearts, words, and conversations. Ultimately, all true prayer and Kingdom activity flow effortlessly from our union with Christ, our redeemed identity, and our conscious awareness of being one with Him.

In this place of union, we experience profound shalom—a peace that doesn't react to earthly circumstances but instead responds directly to Heaven's reality. As conduits of the Kingdom, we live not from earth towards Heaven, but from Heaven towards earth, legislating alignment with Heaven's blueprint. We declare and establish on earth what is already true in Heaven, knowing that Heaven's reality is always intended to become Earth's experience.

Faith doesn't create truth; it recognizes and realizes what is already true. As Bill Johnson beautifully expresses, "Faith actualizes what it realizes" (*The Supernatural Power of a Transformed Mind*, 2005, p. 56). Faith awakens us to the present reality of Heaven, empowering us to manifest and live out the truth we've perceived. Our belief doesn't make something true—it positions us to experience, embody, and release the truth already established in Christ. All genuine faith originates from God; it is not something we muster up in our own strength. Instead, faith is received freely as a divine gift, activated by grace, enabling us to live in continuous alignment with Heaven's reality.

This Kingdom manifestation happens "not by might nor by power, but by My Spirit," says the Lord (Zechariah 4:6, NKJV).

For some, prayer is an afterthought—something done privately or in crisis. At Flō, it is the first step, the guiding force, and the very fabric of how we function. We don't just pray and move forward—we seek Heaven's blueprints first and align everything accordingly.

What happens when a business stops relying on human wisdom alone and begins to function as an Ekklesia—a governing body operating under the divine leadership of Jesus? Everything changes.

? Wonder Questions:

? What if your business meetings became places of prophetic revelation rather than just strategic discussion?

? What if your company operated on supernatural intelligence, not just market trends?

This is the heart of Kingdom living: abiding in God's presence, secure in His goodness, and free to move forward, knowing He works all things together for our good and His glory.

When you engage the spiritual realm as a company, you don't just make good decisions—you walk in divine appointments, supernatural alignment, and Kingdom acceleration.

FLŌ AS A KINGDOM MODEL FOR BUSINESS

This Kingdom atmosphere creates new mindsets filled with abundance, innovation, and creativity that benefit both believers and non-believers alike. It's important to emphasize that the Kingdom is inclusive—everyone experiences its benefits, and people are naturally drawn to the culture of the Kingdom through experiencing the goodness of God. As we embrace this reality, the ties to this world become simultaneously dimmer but also more beautiful and vibrant as we awaken to the limitless reality of heaven and our union with Jesus. Flō has become a prototype for what it looks like when a business becomes an Ekklesia—a governing body of believers executing Heaven's will on Earth. But this isn't just about our company—this is a model for the marketplace and beyond.

Imagine if every business:

🔥 Operated in divine wisdom instead of just human strategy

🔥 Saw employees and leaders functioning in their spiritual gifts

🔥 Became places where Heaven's realities were released into daily operations

The world is waiting for Kingdom businesses—companies that don't just talk about faith but function from Heaven's blueprints.

This is where true Kingdom influence happens.

And the best part... This is just the beginning.

WILL YOU BUILD FROM HEAVEN'S PERSPECTIVE?

The call to ascend isn't just for personal experiences—it's for the transformation of people, families, relationships, businesses, communities, industries, nations, and entire economies.

The Kingdom of God is not just in churches—it is in boardrooms, start-ups, and businesses led by believers who are willing to operate from the Spirit.

If Flō can do it, anyone can.

The only question is:

Will you build your business, your career, and your future from Earth's wisdom or from Heaven's perspective?

The invitation is open.

Will you step in?

BONUS: METANOIA—THE GATEWAY TO ASCENSION

☼ WARNING: This Chapter May Permanently Rewire
Your Spiritual Perception ☼

Proceed with caution (your old way of thinking may not survive the journey)!

Potential side effects include: ✔ Experiencing profound shifts in how you perceive reality ✔ Finding spiritual truths flowing from your spirit rather than just your mind ✔ Developing an unquenchable hunger for deeper union with Christ ✔ Spontaneously seeing life through Heaven's lens rather than earth's limitations

SPIRIT, SOUL, AND BODY: THE FOUNDATION OF ASCENSION

To fully grasp the ascended life, we must first understand the divine architecture of our being. As Paul prays in 1 Thessalonians 5:23 (TPT): "May your entire being—spirit, soul, and body—be kept completely flawless in the appearance of our Lord Jesus, the Anointed One." This three-part design mirrors God's triune nature and holds the key to living from Heaven to earth.

What is metanoia? Far more than "repentance" or "changing your mind," metanoia is a radical revelation that transforms your entire perception of reality to align with God's perspective. It's not a mental exercise but a spiritual awakening that flows from your spirit through your heart and into your mind.

"The goal of the spiritual journey is not to continually search for something that is not present, but to realize who we are and what we've been given in Christ." —Baxter Kruger

Your Spirit — This is your true essence, perfectly one with Christ. The Hebrew word *ruach* conveys both breath and divine life force. Your spirit knows truth instinctively without analysis. "The spirit of man is the lamp of the LORD, searching all his innermost parts" (Proverbs 20:27, ESV). Just as a fiber optic cable carries pure light, your spirit connects directly to God's presence and truth.

Your Heart — Not merely emotions, but the mysterious intersection where spirit and soul meet—the gateway for divine revelation to enter your conscious awareness. This is where true belief forms. Think of your heart as the sacred junction box where heavenly signals are received and distributed to the rest of your being.

Your Soul — Encompasses your mind (thoughts), will (choices), and emotions (feelings). While your spirit is perfectly united with Christ, your soul requires renewal to align with your spiritual reality. Your soul functions like an operating system that needs regular updates to run optimally with the divine source code.

⟡ **Your Mind** — The conscious processing center within your soul. It interprets, analyzes, and communicates what the heart perceives. Your mind is not your brain—your brain is the physical organ through which your mind operates. Similar to how software runs on hardware, your mind processes spiritual data through your physical brain.

Understanding this design reveals why ascension begins with awakening to your spirit's reality rather than mental effort, through a mind in shalom (divine peace). When your mind is at rest, it stops creating static that blocks spirit-to-soul transmission. As Gregory of Nyssa observed, "The intellect cannot see the things of God until it is set free and enlightened by the Holy Spirit" (*On the Soul and the Resurrection*, 4th century).

This spiritual architecture explains why we often "know" truth in our spirit before we can articulate it with our mind. Ascension flows from spirit to mind—never mind to spirit. Like a well-engineered system, when each component functions according to its design specifications, the whole operates with divine efficiency.

THE SANCTIFIED IMAGINATION: HEAVEN'S GATEWAY IN YOUR MIND

Between your spirit's heavenly position and your mind's earthly experience lies a powerful tool often misunderstood—your imagination. Far from mere fantasy, your sanctified imagination is a God-given faculty designed to help you perceive spiritual realities.

♦ *What Imagination Really Is*—Your imagination isn't just the ability to create mental pictures—it's the capacity to perceive what exists beyond physical sight. It's a receiving antenna, not merely a projector of your own thoughts.

Think of your imagination as a bridge between realms—a place where your spirit can communicate heavenly realities to your mind. When surrendered to the Holy Spirit, your imagination becomes one of the primary ways you receive divine impressions, visions, and revelations.

As C.S. Lewis wrote, "Reason is the natural organ of truth; imagination is the organ of meaning" (*Bluspels and Flalansferes*, 1939). Your rational mind processes information, but your imagination grasps significance and reality beyond mere facts.

♦ *From Religious Fear to Divine Function*—Many believers hesitate to engage their imagination in spiritual matters, fearing deception or "making things up." This fear stems from a misunderstanding of how God designed us to perceive spiritual realities.

Scripture repeatedly shows God using visual language to communicate: Ezekiel's visions, John's apocalyptic imagery, and Jesus' parables all engaged the imagination to convey heavenly truth. God meets us in our capacity to visualize and perceive beyond the visible.

When Paul prays for "the eyes of your heart to be enlightened" (Ephesians 1:18, NIV) he's referencing this spiritual-perceptual capacity— your imagination baptized in truth.

♦ *Practical Imagination Training*—Like any faculty, your spiritual imagination develops with practice:

1. Start by visualizing scriptural truths—see yourself seated with Christ (Ephesians 2:6, NKJV)

2. When praying, allow mental images to form without forcing or directing them

3. Notice the difference between images you consciously create versus those that arise spontaneously

4. Keep a journal of impressions, paying attention to patterns and confirmations

5. Test everything against Scripture and in community

In ascension, you're not creating imaginary scenarios—you're allowing your imagination to become a lens through which you perceive heavenly realities that already exist. As your imagination aligns with truth, Heaven's perspective becomes your natural way of seeing.

THE TRANSFORMATIVE POWER OF RENEWED THINKING

The ancient Greek word for "transformed" in Romans 12:2 is metamorphoō—the same word used for Jesus' transfiguration. This isn't a slight improvement but a complete metamorphosis, like a caterpillar becoming a butterfly.

"Be inwardly transformed by the Holy Spirit through a total reformation of how you think. This will empower you to discern God's will as you live a beautiful life, satisfying, and perfect in his eyes" (Romans 12:2, TPT).

This transformation follows a divine pathway:

1. Revelation begins in your spirit

2. Illuminates your heart

3. Reshapes your mind

4. Transforms your actions

5. Manifests in the physical world

True metanoia works like waking from a dream. When dreaming, the dream world seems completely real. No amount of analysis within the dream can wake you. But upon awakening, your perspective shifts instantly—you simply know the dream wasn't real.

WHY METANOIA IS ESSENTIAL FOR ASCENSION

◆ From Thinking to Seeing—Metanoia shifts you from trying to think your way into truth to simply seeing truth as it is. It means a complete transformation of our thinking to align with God's perspective.

◆ From Striving to Rest—Instead of mental effort, faith becomes the effortless response to unveiled reality.

◆ From Information to Revelation—You move from accumulated knowledge to infused revelation—truth that flows from your union with Christ.

The difficulty many experience with ascension is attempting it from the mind rather than the spirit. When you try to ascend through mental techniques alone, you hit a ceiling. But when ascension flows from your spirit—where you're already seated with Christ—Heaven's realities naturally manifest.

PRACTICAL STEPS TO EXPERIENCE METANOIA

1. *Surrender Your Mind*—Acknowledge that your spirit, not your mind, is designed to lead. "The intellect cannot see the things of God until it is set free by the Holy Spirit."

2. *Engage in Spirit*—First Practices—Worship, contemplative prayer, and Scripture meditation engage your spirit directly with God's Spirit.

3. *Pay Attention to Heart-Knowing*—Notice those moments when you simply "know" something without figuring it out. This is your spirit communicating through your heart.

4. *Renew Subconscious Patterns*—As you align with divine truth, allow it to reshape your deeply held beliefs and automatic responses.

5. *Live From Union, Not Toward It*—Recognize that transformation is not about becoming something new but awakening to who you've always been in Christ.

⟡ ASCENSION ACTIVATION ⟡

Take a moment to close your eyes and declare aloud: "I am spirit, not mind. My thoughts do not define me; my oneness with Christ does. I allow my spirit to lead as I align with Heaven's perspective."

Feel the shift from mental striving to spiritual awareness. This is the foundation for true ascension—living from the spirit, not just the mind.

THE SPIRIT-LED ASCENSION

When we understand our design as spirit, soul, and body, ascension becomes natural—not a struggle, but a joyful recognition of our position in Christ. We don't ascend to reach Heaven; we ascend because we're already seated there.

This is metanoia—the radical shift in perception that opens the gateway to Heaven's realities. It empowers us to discern God's will and live beautiful, satisfying lives that perfectly reflect His nature.

> ✅ You are spirit, not mind ✅ Metanoia flows from spirit to mind which is in shalom, at rest, not mind to spirit ✅ Faith is the response to unveiled truth, not mental effort ✅ Transformation comes through awareness, not striving ✅ The aroma of Christ flows naturally from your true identity

As you embrace this truth, you'll find that ascension isn't about straining to reach higher—it's about awakening to where you already are, seated with Christ in heavenly places.

CHAPTER 3: ✦🔥 SEATED WITH CHRIST

Side effects may include: ✅ Finding yourself looking down at problems instead of up at them ✅ Spontaneously declaring truth instead of begging for answers ✅ Experiencing supernatural peace in situations that used to cause anxiety

LIVING FROM THE THRONE ROOM OF GOD

If you are seated with Christ in heavenly places, how does this change everything about the way you live, think, and engage with the world?

The practice of ascension—engaging with the heavenly realms—unlocks new dimensions of spiritual authority, revelation, and transformation. But here's the key:

🔥 Ascension isn't about leaving earth; it's about fully stepping into the divine reality that has always been available to you.

You were never meant to live from below. You were always meant to rise.

THE FOUNDATION OF REST & GRACE: THE POSTURE OF ASCENSION

You have been known and loved since before time began. Before the foundations of the world, you were chosen in Him—designed to dwell in unbroken union with God. You were never created for striving; you were created for rest.

This foundational truth echoes what Irenaeus of Lyon expressed in the second century: "The glory of God is a human being fully alive" (*Against Heresies*, Book IV, 20:7). For Irenaeus, our true glory wasn't found in religious effort but in the fullness of divine life flowing through us. We were created for communion, not performance.

The fall introduced sin-consciousness that kept humanity trapped in the deception that we had to 'earn' our way back to God. But in reality, salvation is not a transaction that can be earned through good behavior or performance. It is entirely based on grace through the finished work of the cross—there is absolutely nothing we can add to it!

While we were still dead in our sin, Jesus died for us, made us alive in Him, raised us up, and seated us with Him in heavenly places (Ephesians 2:5-6). This gift of grace completely transforms our relationship with God from one of striving to one of receiving.

As Augustine wrote in his *Confessions*, "You have made us for yourself, O Lord, and our hearts are restless until they rest in you" (*Confessions*, Book I, 1). This restlessness isn't resolved through striving but through awakening to the rest that has always been our inheritance in Christ.

? Wonder Question:

? How might your approach to spiritual growth shift if you truly believed you don't need to earn God's love or presence?

"Now, if anyone is enfolded into Christ, he has become an entirely new person. All that is related to the old order has vanished. Behold, everything is fresh and new." —2 Corinthians 5:17 (TPT)

The old world of striving has been erased. You now stand in the fullness of His righteousness, completely reconciled. The key to ascension is living from the awareness of divine union rather than the illusion of distance.

THE REALITY OF BEING SEATED WITH CHRIST

"He raised us up with Christ the exalted One, and we ascended with him into the glorious perfection and authority of the heavenly realm, for we are now co-seated as one with Christ!" —Ephesians 2:6 (TPT)

We simply can't hear this enough! This isn't a promise for some distant future—it's your present-day reality. You are not waiting to ascend; you've already ascended! In Christ, you are positioned in divine authority and glory right now. Embrace this profound truth, live from this heavenly perspective, and watch as it transforms every area of your life today.

Cyril of Alexandria, in the 5th century, understood this profound truth when he wrote: "Christ did not ascend alone, but we also ascended with Him. For since He comes from us, from our nature... we are all in Christ" (*Commentary on John*, Book 11, Chapter 11). For Cyril, our ascension wasn't a future hope but a present reality secured in Christ's own ascension.

✅ You govern from Heaven, not react from earth.

✅ You pray from victory, not struggle toward it.

✅ You release Heaven's realities, rather than wait for permission.

For too long, the Church has focused on "getting to Heaven one day" instead of realizing that Heaven is already within us.

Jesus said:

"The kingdom is not discovered in one place or another, for God's kingdom realm is already expanding within some of you." —Luke 17:21 (TPT)

🔥 Ascension is the practice of aligning with this truth.

🚪 You are already inside the throne room. The only thing required is awareness.

ASCENSION ACTIVATION: THRONE ROOM AWARENESS

The Biblical Foundation of the Throne Room

In Revelation 4, John provides us with a stunning glimpse into Heaven's throne room:

"After this I looked, and there before me was a door standing open in Heaven. And the voice I had first heard speaking to me like a trumpet said, 'Come up here, and I will show you what must take place after this.' At once I was in the Spirit, and there before me was a throne in Heaven with someone sitting on it. And the one who sat there had the appearance of jasper and ruby. A rainbow that shone like an emerald encircled the throne." —Revelation 4:1-3 (NKJV) (NIV)

John goes on to describe:

- Twenty-four elders dressed in white, wearing crowns of gold
- Flashes of lightning and rumblings of thunder
- A sea of glass, clear as crystal
- Four living creatures surrounding the throne
- Continuous worship declaring "Holy, holy, holy is the Lord God Almighty, who was, and is, and is to come" (Revelation 4:8, NKJV)

This wasn't merely a vision for John. It was an invitation to experience the reality of Heaven—an invitation that extends to every believer today.

This isn't future tense—it's your current reality. You don't need to strive to access the throne room; you simply need to awaken to the truth that you are already there in Christ.

Now, I invite you to experience this reality through a guided practice:

1. Find a quiet place where you won't be disturbed for at least fifteen minutes.

2. Assume a comfortable position, either sitting or lying down, with your spine straight but relaxed.

3. Begin with three deep breaths, inhaling peace and exhaling any tension or distractions.

4. Declare your position: "Through the finished work of Christ, I am already seated with Him in heavenly places. I have full access

to the throne room of God, not by my own merit, but through my union with Jesus."

5. Engage your sanctified imagination: Picture yourself entering through an open door in Heaven, just as John did. See yourself stepping into an atmosphere charged with glory, where colors are more vibrant than any on earth and the air itself seems alive with the presence of God.

6. Come into the awareness that the throne room is within, not a far away place.

7. Behold the throne: See the magnificent throne at the center of the room, encircled by an emerald rainbow. The one seated there radiates light so brilliant it's almost beyond comprehension—like jasper and ruby. Don't strain to see details clearly; simply rest in the awareness of His presence.

8. Notice the atmosphere: Feel the weightless joy and perfect peace that permeates this place. The air itself seems to pulse with love, wisdom, and power. There is no fear here, only perfect love and acceptance.

9. Recognize your position: See yourself seated with Christ, not as a visitor or guest, but as a beloved child who belongs, filled with awe and wonder, living in the present moment. This is your rightful place, secured by the blood of Jesus. Come into awareness of your union with Christ—oneness.

10. Participate in the worship: Hear the continuous declarations of "Holy, holy, holy" coming from the four living creatures. Let your heart join this eternal worship, not from a place of religious duty, but from genuine awe at His majesty.

11. Receive impartation: As you rest in this place, allow the atmosphere of heaven to fill you completely. Feel your perceptions

being aligned with Heaven's reality. Let divine perspective saturate your thoughts, emotions, and even your physical body.

12. Listen for His voice: In this place of perfect communion, be attentive to any words, impressions, or Scriptures that come to mind. The Holy Spirit may highlight specific areas of your life where Heaven's reality needs to manifest.

13. Record your experience: When you're ready to conclude, gently return your awareness to your physical surroundings. Take a few moments to journal about what you saw, felt, heard, or sensed during this time.

MAKING THIS YOUR DAILY REALITY

The power of this practice isn't found in a one-time experience but in making it part of your daily consciousness. Here are some practical ways to strengthen your throne room awareness:

- *Begin each day with a declaration*: Before your feet hit the floor in the morning, declare "I am seated with Christ in heavenly places today."

- *Create triggers throughout your day*: Use ordinary moments (stopping at a red light, washing your hands, drinking water) as reminders to shift your awareness to your heavenly position.

- *Reframe challenges*: When facing difficult situations, ask yourself, "How does this look from the throne room perspective?"

- *Practice corporate ascension*: Find others who are exploring these realities and spend time ascending together.

- *Live from Heaven to earth:* Instead of praying for Heaven to come down, live as though you're releasing Heaven's realities from your position of authority.

Remember, this isn't about achieving a special spiritual state—it's about awakening to what has always been true of you in Christ. The veil has been torn, the door stands open, and your place is secured.

What would change in your life if you lived every moment from the awareness of being seated with Christ in the throne room? That's the invitation before you now.

Will you step in?

What Scripture calls 'unapproachable light' (1 Timothy 6:16) has been described in various traditions, including by some Jewish scholars, as 'Ain Soph Aur' or 'Endless Light'—the boundless radiance of God's presence.

AIN SOPH AUR: THE FULLNESS OF LIGHT AND ASCENSION

Ain Soph Aur—translated as Endless Light—describes the infinite, uncreated radiance of God. It represents the boundless divine presence that fills all things, the pure essence of God's being beyond time and space.

This concept is deeply intertwined with ascension, because ascension is stepping into the light of divine reality.

Dionysius the Areopagite, in his *Mystical Theology*, described divine light as simultaneously "dazzling darkness" and "brilliant light"—a paradox that captures the overwhelming reality of God's presence that both blinds and illuminates (Mystical Theology, Chapter 1). For Dionysius, ascension was the journey into this divine light that ultimately transcends all human categories and concepts.

Consider our sun, the vibrant star that sustains life on earth. It is approximately 400,000 times brighter than the most powerful industrial floodlight. Its intensity can overwhelm our vision if stared at directly even for a moment. Now consider quasars, cosmic beacons powered by super-massive black holes, emitting brightness billions of times greater than our sun—so powerful they outshine entire galaxies. Yet, even these celestial marvels are mere shadows compared to the dazzling, uncreated brilliance of Ain Soph Aur, the Endless Light of God's presence.

LIGHT AS THE ULTIMATE TRANSFORMATIONAL AGENT

What's remarkable about light—even at the quantum level—is that photons serve as nature's perfect transitioning agents. Einstein's revelations about the photon showed us that light exists as both particle and wave simultaneously, transcending our normal categories of existence. Photons transform matter, catalyze chemical reactions, and literally change the substance of what they touch. They don't merely illuminate objects—they fundamentally alter them.

This quantum reality reflects a profound spiritual truth: divine light doesn't just reveal; it transforms. When we encounter the Endless Light of God's presence, we aren't merely seeing more clearly—we're being fundamentally changed at the deepest level of our being. The photon's ability to exist beyond time (as Einstein showed) mirrors how God's light transcends our temporal reality, inviting us into eternity even while we remain in time.

Jesus manifests this light fully:

"I am the Light to the world and those who embrace Me will experience life-giving light, and they will never walk in darkness." (John 8:12, TPT)

The Kingdom of Light is not something we attain—it is something we awaken to.

As Justin Paul Abraham teaches, when we engage with this divine light through ascension, we step into what he calls "the bliss of knowing"—

an encounter with God's presence that transcends intellectual understanding and brings us into experiential knowledge of our true identity in Christ (*Burning Ones*, 2016, p. 87).

Paul affirms this:

"Feast on all the treasures of the heavenly realm and fill your thoughts with heavenly realities, and not with the distractions of the natural realm. Your crucifixion with Christ has severed the tie to this life, and now your true life is hidden away in God in Christ." (Colossians 3:2-3, TPT)

Ain Soph Aur is the full revelation of Christ's divine presence—it is the substance of Heaven itself.

In this light, ascension becomes a daily act of stepping into the radiant presence of God—a revelation of Christ's fullness. Ain Soph Aur is not merely a metaphor; it is the substance of Heaven itself, a living expression of divine energy, wisdom, and love. Just as photons transform everything they touch, this divine light transforms us from within, not just illuminating our path but fundamentally changing our spiritual DNA into glory.

FAITH, NOT WORKS: CHANTAL'S RESPONSE

I once heard the phrase, "faith bypasses works." While faith without works is dead, if we don't know the intention of God's heart, we could easily get caught up in wrong works, religious acts, or legalistic rituals. We could easily go down the wrong path.

This understanding parallels what Augustine meant when he said, "Love God and do what you please" (*Homilies on 1 John*, 7:8). When we are rooted in divine love and faith, our actions naturally flow from that place of union rather than religious obligation.

That's why Jesus said:

"The work you can do for God starts with believing in the One He has sent." —John 6:29 (TPT)

Our old or false identity has been crucified with Christ. Now, the life we live is empowered by the faith of the Son of God, who loves us and gave His life for us (Galatians 2:19-20, TPT).

We must get out of the way and let His Kingdom come through us! God is seeking those whose hearts fully belong to Him. It's not by might or power, but by His Spirit.

He desires to exceed our wildest dreams!

This is ascension:

- *Not striving, but faith receiving.*
- *Not religious effort, but alignment with divine reality.*
- *Not earning, but awakened sonship.*

From this foundation, Chantal's testimony flows as a real-life example of faith bypassing works.

AIN SOPH AUR AND THE MYSTICAL REALITY OF ASCENSION

Ain Soph Aur represents more than just divine light—it is the energy, wisdom, and supernatural flow of Heaven itself.

Throughout ascension experiences, believers often describe:

Waves of liquid light—the tangible, radiant presence of God.

Swirling circles of energy—the dynamic movement of the Spirit.

Orbs of divine presence—portals opening into new realms of encounter.

Waterfalls of heavenly outpouring—the continuous cascade of divine love, wisdom, and empowerment.

These descriptions echo what Hildegard of Bingen recorded in her visions: "The light which I see is not bound by space ... It is far, far brighter than a cloud which carries the sun" (*Scivias*, Book I, Vision 1, 12th century). Hildegard experienced divine light not as static but as dynamic, flowing, and alive—qualities that modern believers continue to encounter in ascension experiences.

This aligns with biblical imagery of heavenly realms:

"The throne of God is surrounded by an emerald rainbow—a full circle of light, symbolizing unbroken divinity." —Revelation 4:2-6 (TPT)

"God is Light, and in Him there is no darkness at all." —1 John 1:5 (TPT)

Jesus is the bridge (door or fusion) between Ain Soph Aur and ascension:

"I am the Way, the Truth, and the Life..." —John 14:6 (TPT)

We do not work our way into divine light—we step into the revelation that we are already in it.

Ain Soph Aur, thus, not only embodies divine illumination but represents the believer's ultimate calling: to dwell continuously in God's endless light, wisdom, and energy. Through ascension, believers awaken to the transformative reality of Ain Soph Aur—living beyond earthly limits, immersed in the perpetual waterfall of God's presence.

LIGHT, WISDOM, AND IMMORTAL ENERGY IN ASCENSION

When we engage in ascension, we are not just stepping into knowledge—we are stepping into divine wisdom and immortal energy.

Light——Represents revelation, divine illumination, and hidden realms unveiled.

Pseudo—Dionysius taught that divine light operates hierarchically, flowing from God through various celestial orders and ultimately to humans (Celestial Hierarchy, Chapter 1, 5th century). In ascension, we experience this illuminating light directly, which transforms our perception and understanding.

Wisdom (Chokmah in Hebrew)——Divine wisdom is imparted through encounters with God. Jesus is the Wisdom of God (1 Corinthians 1:24, TPT).

Maximus the Confessor described wisdom as "the knowledge of divine and human matters and their causes" (*Centuries on Knowledge*, 1:9, 7th century). For Maximus, this wisdom wasn't merely intellectual but experiential—the fruit of divine encounter that transforms our entire being.

Immortal Energy——In Christ, we already have eternal life. Ascension dismantles the illusion of limitation and mortality and awakens us to divine reality.

Gregory Palamas, in the 14th century, taught about the "uncreated energies" of God—divine operations through which God becomes knowable to human beings while remaining transcendent in His essence (*Triads*, I.3.38). These energies, according to Palamas, are how we experience divine life and participate in eternity.

This is why ascension is necessary—it reorients us from earthly limitation to divine flow.

"For our spiritual wealth is in Him, like hidden treasure waiting to be discovered—heaven's wisdom and endless riches of revelation knowledge." —Colossians 2:3 (TPT)

As Nancy Cohen has described in her teachings on heavenly realms, engaging with the light and wisdom of God enables us to access divine revelation that transcends human understanding (*Keys to Heaven's Economy*, 2009, p. 43). She explains that when we step into ascension, we tap into the same reality experienced by the apostle John when he was "in the Spirit" and received the revelations recorded in the book of Revelation.

As early Christian mystic Gregory of Nyssa wrote, "The soul's ascent to God is limitless because the One whom the soul seeks is beyond all limitation" (*Life of Moses*, 4th century, Book II.239). This ancient understanding affirms what we're experiencing today—ascension is the journey of awakening to infinite divine reality.

✦ACTIVATION: STEP INTO THE LIGHT ✦

This is not just knowledge—this is an invitation into an encounter.

1 Close your eyes.

2 Picture yourself standing before Jesus as He radiates light.

3 Step into His presence and allow His glory to envelop you.

4 Feel the warmth of Ain Soph Aur—the uncreated light of God.

5 Allow the Spirit to reveal wisdom, insight, and divine energy to you.

This practice mirrors what Symeon the New Theologian described as "the experience of divine light"—a direct, personal encounter with God's radiance that transforms the believer from within (Discourses, 22, 10th century). For Symeon, this wasn't mere visualization but actual participation in divine reality.

? **Wonder Questions:**

? What do you see in the light of God's presence?

? How does it feel to simply receive rather than strive?

? What new truths become clear when viewed through Heaven's light?

? How might this experience transform your daily walk?

This is the reality of ascension.

A NEW SEASON OF PRAYER: CHANTAL'S RESPONSE

In 2010, I began spending hours in God's presence after my children left for school. My husband would come home and ask, "What did you do today?" I would simply reply, "I spent hours with the Lord." He would joke, "It would be great if you could get paid for that!"

Little did we know, God was about to make that happen.

One Sunday, I shared a dream with a friend at church, and he exclaimed, "You're the one! You're the person we've been praying to hire." They had been seeking a "prayer person" for their film company, and that dream confirmed it. Shortly after, I became a spiritual advisor and intercessor for the company.

This experience mirrors the journey of Julian of Norwich, who devoted herself to prayer and subsequently received divine visions that she was called to share with others (*Revelations of Divine Love*, Chapter 2, 14th century). Like Julian, Chantal's private devotion became a public ministry, confirming that what we receive in the secret place is often meant to impact others.

God had set me on a path, and there was no turning back.

CHANTAL'S MARKETPLACE CALLING & THE WHITE KEY

In 2016, a businessman walked into the prayer room and started fellow-shipping with us. He later invited a group of us to form a prayer team for his company.

Little did I know that I would become a close friend, walking with Bryan through a long journey of transformation and growth.

Early in our journey together, the Lord gave me a dream of a white key that Bryan gave me.

In the dream, I found myself walking through the streets of Toronto while Bryan was teaching me about business. I was receiving divine knowledge and training. I was also shown that God would gather the blueprints of Heaven and that everything would come together. Bryan came to me in the dream and gave me a white key.

The white key symbolized:

🔑 Authority to unlock spiritual and natural dimensions.

🔑 Light and purity—a Kingdom assignment.

🔑 Heaven's wisdom—God's divine strategies for marketplace influence.

This vision of a key echoes the ancient Christian symbol of the "keys of the kingdom" that Christ gave to Peter. Throughout Christian history, keys have represented divine authority and access to heavenly realities. As Ambrose of Milan wrote in the 4th century, "What are the keys of the kingdom of heaven? They are faith and authority" (*Concerning Repentance*, Book I, Chapter 1).

This dream confirmed that we were being aligned with divine blue-prints—where spiritual revelation would govern natural realities.

"We have become His poetry, a re-created people that will fulfill the destiny He has given each of us, for we are joined to Jesus, the Anointed One." —Ephesians 2:10 (TPT)

LIVING FROM HEAVEN'S PERSPECTIVE: BRYAN'S INSIGHTS

As I've journeyed deeper into the reality of being seated with Christ, I've noticed how it transforms my approach to leadership, decision-making, and even problem-solving. When challenges arise in our business, I no longer see them from a purely earthly perspective.

Instead, I find myself stepping back and viewing situations from a heavenly vantage point. This shift in perspective brings clarity, wisdom, and an awareness of divine solutions that weren't visible from below. The pressures and anxieties that once consumed me now seem distant and manageable, as I govern from a place of rest rather than struggle. Shalom!

This heavenly perspective reflects what Clement of Alexandria called "the eye of the soul" that perceives divine realities (*Stromata*, Book V, Chapter 1, 3rd century). Clement taught that when this spiritual eye is purified and awakened, we begin to see not just with natural sight but with the vision of Christ.

In practical terms, this looks like beginning each day with the awareness of my union. From this position, I approach meetings, conversations, and decisions with the awareness that I have access to divine insight and supernatural intelligence. The results have been transformative, not just for me personally, but for our entire organization.

Liz Wright describes this posture beautifully when she teaches about "living loved from above." She explains that when we truly grasp our identity as beloved children seated with Christ, we begin to manifest Kingdom realities naturally, without striving (*Heaven on Earth*, 2018, p.

89). This is exactly what I've experienced—the more I rest in my heavenly position, the more heavenly wisdom and authority flow through me.

This is the difference between trying to access Heaven and living from the revelation that we're already there. It's not about achieving a higher state—it's about awakening to where we've always been positioned in Christ. When we see from this perspective, everything changes.

ASCENSION ACTIVATION: STEP INTO THE HEAVENLIES

Ascension is not a theory—it is an experience. Let's step into it now:

1 Close your eyes.

2 See yourself seated with Christ in the heavenly places.

3 Ask the Holy Spirit: What do You want me to see?

4 Let His presence surround you. Feel the light of Heaven wash over you.

This practice resembles what the Eastern Church calls "noetic prayer"— prayer that engages not just the intellect but the nous, the spiritual faculty that perceives divine realities. As Theophan the Recluse taught, "The principal thing is to stand with the mind in the heart before God, and to go on standing before Him unceasingly day and night, until the end of life" (*The Art of Prayer*, 1965, p. 63).

 What do you see? Hear? Experience?

This is not imagination—it is spiritual sight. The more you practice this, the more tangible it becomes.

As Bill Johnson teaches, "The primary function of the believer is to make the invisible Kingdom visible" (*When Heaven Invades Earth*, 2003, p. 38). This activation helps train your spiritual senses to perceive and then demonstrate heavenly realities on earth.

PRACTICAL APPLICATION: LIVING SEATED WITH CHRIST

How does the truth of being seated with Christ transform your daily life? Here are some practical areas where this reality can make a profound difference:

Decision-Making- When faced with choices, large or small, take a moment to shift your awareness to your seated position with Christ. From this vantage point, ask for Heaven's perspective. What does divine wisdom reveal about this situation?

Try This: Before your next important decision, close your eyes and picture yourself seated next to Jesus, looking at the situation together. Ask, "Lord, how do You see this?"

This approach mirrors what Ignatius of Loyola called "discernment of spirits"—the practice of perceiving God's movement and direction in everyday decisions (*Spiritual Exercises, Rules for Discernment*, 16th century). For Ignatius, this wasn't just about making good choices, but about aligning every decision with divine purpose.

Conflict Resolution: When tensions arise, step back and view the conflict from your heavenly position. From above, you can see past temporary emotions to the hearts involved and the Kingdom's purposes at stake.

Try This: In your next difficult conversation, pause, and silently declare, "I am seated with Christ above this situation." Notice how your perspective shifts.

Prayer and Intercession: Instead of praying from a place of need or lack, pray from the awareness that you are already in the heavenlies. Declare Heaven's realities rather than begging for them.

Try This: Begin your prayers with "As one seated with Christ, I declare..." instead of "Please God, would You..."

This approach to prayer reflects what John Cassian taught in the 5th century about "pure prayer"—prayer that moves beyond petitions to a direct communion with God, where our hearts align with His and our declarations flow from that unity (*Conferences*, 9:18).

Identity and Purpose: Allow the truth of being seated with Christ to define who you are and why you're here. Your purpose flows from your position, not from earthly expectations or achievements.

Try This: Write down three ways your life would change if you consistently lived from your heavenly position rather than your earthly circumstances.

Rest and Peace: When life feels overwhelming, remember that you are seated far above every problem and challenge. Let this truth anchor your heart in supernatural peace.

Try This: When anxiety rises, place your hand on your heart and whisper, "I am seated with Christ above this storm."

START HERE: THREE DAILY PRACTICES

Not sure how to begin living from your heavenly position? Try these three simple practices this week:

- *Morning Position Declaration (30 seconds)* Before getting out of bed each morning, declare: "I am seated with Christ in heavenly places today. I see from Heaven's perspective."

- *Midday Perspective Shift (2 minutes)* Set a reminder on your phone for midday. When it goes off, pause, and ask: "Jesus, how do You see the situation I'm in right now?" Then listen.

- *Evening Light Immersion (5 minutes)* Before sleep, imagine yourself surrounded by God's light. No agenda, no requests—just rest in His presence and receive.

? **Wonder Questions:**

? What if the veil between Heaven and earth isn't just thin—it has been torn wide open.

? How would you approach today differently if you truly believed you had full access to Heaven's perspective and resources right now?

? What if your ordinary Monday morning could be experienced while fully aware of your seated position with Christ?

? How might your commute, your meetings, or your family dinner be transformed? Every moment is holy to God!

? What if the challenges you're facing right now look completely different from Heaven's perspective?

? What solutions might become visible if you viewed them from your seated position with Christ?

☺ REFLECTION QUESTIONS:

? How would your approach to prayer change if you truly believed you were already seated with Christ in the heavenly places?

? In what areas of your life do you still find yourself striving rather than resting in your heavenly position?

? What would it look like for you to govern from Heaven in your sphere of influence (family, workplace, ministry)?

? How might the awareness of being surrounded by Ain Soph Aur (God's endless light) transform your perception of yourself and others?

? What practical steps can you take this week to align your daily life with the reality of your heavenly position?

You were never meant to live from below but as a multi-locational being made in the image of God.

AWAKENING TO YOUR BI-LOCATIONAL, MULTI-DIMENSIONAL REALITY

In Chantal's own words:

One of the most transformative revelations I've received is discovering that we are far more than just physical beings. Created in God's image, we have capacities that extend beyond our natural understanding.

In dreams and visions, I've participated in cosmic missions—interacting with planets and realms beyond Earth while my body slept. These weren't mere imaginations but genuine experiences where my spirit was engaged with realities that exist in God's vast creation.

This understanding brings a new perspective on scriptures like Paul's experience of being 'caught up to the third heaven' (2 Corinthians 12:2 (NKJV)) or John being 'in the Spirit on the Lord's day' (Revelation 1:10). These weren't exceptional experiences reserved for apostles—they reflect our inherent design as spiritual beings.

When you step out of the limitations of your body/soul awareness, you can interface with numerous dimensions and beings that exist in God. I've come to understand that 'angels' is a broad term encompassing many types of living creatures that inhabit different realms of God's creation.

Each encounter leaves me with a deeper sense of wonder at God's creative genius and the dignity He has bestowed upon humanity by making us in His image—with capacities that mirror His own multi-dimensional nature.

In this higher reality, we discover the profound truth that Julian of Norwich captured in her *Revelation of Divine Love* (14th century): "All shall be well, and all shall be well, and all manner of thing shall be well." This isn't wishful thinking but the highest truth of the Kingdom of God— an internal reality we can rest in regardless of external circumstances.

The most beautiful aspect is realizing this is who we've always been. In Christ, we're not becoming something new—we're awakening to what has always been true of us as an image-bearer of a limitless God.

🔥 You were always meant to rise.

The invitation stands. *Will you ascend?*

CHAPTER 4: ✦🔥 REVELATION— LIVING FROM DIVINE PERSPECTIVE

🚨 WARNING: This Chapter May Permanently Upgrade
Your Spiritual Vision 🚨

Side effects may include: ✅ Seeing solutions where you once saw only problems ✅ Recognizing God's voice in places you've been missing it ✅ Finding yourself declaring Heaven's reality instead of accepting earth's limitations

❓ What if God has been speaking all along, but we've been listening with the wrong ears?

In the journey of Kingdom living, we're called to follow Jesus' example of perfect unity with the Father. When Jesus said, "I only do what I see the Father doing" (John 5:19), He wasn't sharing a spiritual technique— He was revealing a lifestyle of heavenly perception that transformed everything.

This is the essence of spiritual ascension: shifting from human reasoning to divine awareness.

THE CALL TO ASCENDED REVELATION

Revelation isn't merely knowledge—it's an awakening to divine reality. When we understand that Jesus lived from the unseen realm, governing from above, it challenges us to do the same. This doesn't mean we ignore earthly life; it means we approach it from a heavenly vantage point.

Colossians 3:1-3 (TPT) instructs us to "yearn for all that is above, for that's where Christ sits enthroned at the place of all power, honor, and authority! Yes, feast on all the treasures of the heavenly realm and fill your thoughts with heavenly realities, and not with the distractions of the natural realm. Your crucifixion with Christ has severed the tie to this life, and now your true life is hidden away in God in Christ." The more we align with the mind of Christ, the more revelation flows—transforming how we think, act, and bring Heaven to earth.

? Wonder Questions:

? When was the last time you received a divine insight that completely changed how you approached a situation?

? How did this "seeing from above" transform your understanding?

CONTEMPLATIVE PRAYER: SIMPLY BEING WITH GOD

"Be still, and know that I am God." —Psalm 46:10 (NIV)

Ascension is beautifully interwoven with the gentle, quiet posture of contemplative prayer. Unlike prayer as we often understand it—filled with speaking, requesting, and seeking—contemplative prayer invites us into the profound simplicity of silence and stillness before God. This practice isn't about reaching for spiritual experiences or ascending through our efforts. Instead, it's about recognizing and resting in the reality that we are already seated with Christ in heavenly places (Ephesians 2:6, NKJV).

Jeanne Guyon, the French mystic, describes contemplative prayer beautifully: "Prayer is nothing else but the application of the heart to God, and the interior exercise of love" (*A Short Method of Prayer*, 1685, p. 2). She teaches that true intimacy with God comes not through striving but through a quiet surrender, a gentle letting go of self and a simple resting in God's presence. Guyon further states, "It is only by a total death to self we can be lost in God" (*Spiritual Torrents*, 1682, p. 48), emphasizing that contemplative prayer is about selfless communion and surrender rather than seeking personal gain.

Gene Ganiel also describes contemplative prayer as a "prayer of silence," emphasizing its essence as simply standing in solitude in the secret place with God. She highlights that in contemplative prayer, we are not looking for experiences or revelations; we are there solely to be present with God. This form of prayer recenters us, drawing us back into the peaceful truth that He is restoring all things, including our souls.

Brother Lawrence echoes this beautifully: "I have quit all forms of devotion and set prayers but those to which my state obliges me. My only business now is persevering in His presence... a simple attention and a general fond regard to God" (*The Practice of the Presence of God*, 1691, p. 19). Contemplative prayer is precisely this simple attention. It is consciously offering our silence and gratitude to Him, fully confident in His presence and goodness.

Contemplative prayer is also a beautiful form of meditation, similar to focusing on our breath. Just as breath meditation centers and calms the body, contemplative prayer quiets our soul and creates space for our spirit to commune deeply with God. This practice is an essential and beneficial spiritual discipline for Christians, demonstrating that intentional stillness before God is not only compatible with our faith but central to it.

When thoughts arise, we don't cling to them; we gently let them pass, returning to a quiet focus on God. We're not performing or striving but resting in the assured comfort that He is here, with us, always.

This prayer of silence invites us into deeper intimacy with the Father, not through action but through surrender. It is not an exercise or a process, but a state of being—a state in which our souls quietly acknowledge the loving presence of our Creator. Through this humble posture, we begin to embody the peace and rest of Heaven itself, realizing that His kingdom is not something distant to be sought, but a present reality to be embraced. This opens us to see God in everything as we awaken.

☙ Reflective Question:

? How does the idea of simply being with God, rather than striving for an encounter, reshape your approach to prayer and intimacy with Him?

THE SCIENCE OF SACRED BREATHING: NEURAL INTEGRATION AND SPIRITUAL ACTIVATION

Recent groundbreaking research has unveiled an extraordinary link between our breathing patterns and brain function, particularly emphasizing the role of cannabinoid receptors within our body's endocannabinoid system. These receptors are crucial players in the brain's salience network, a neural circuit integral to coordinating attention, cognitive processes, and emotional regulation.

When we practice mindful, rhythmic breathing—such as Trinitarian breathing or other sacred breathing methods—we directly activate these cannabinoid receptors. This activation sets off a chain reaction of physiological events, fostering greater integration and coherence across various neural networks. The synchronization of these networks is instrumental in promoting a profound state of internal harmony and physiological peace.

Simply put, conscious breathing acts as a natural biological "switch" that engages the body's inherent systems designed for harmony and balance. As we inhale deeply and intentionally, these cannabinoid receptors respond by enhancing communication between different brain regions, significantly reducing stress responses and creating an optimal environment for spiritual sensitivity and awareness.

Conscious breathing also increases interoceptive focus—our ability to sense internal bodily sensations—enabling us to be more still, attentive, and receptive to the subtle voice and presence of God. This state of enhanced internal awareness facilitates deeper listening, reflection, and spiritual discernment.

This scientific insight offers biological confirmation of what spiritual practitioners have intuitively understood for centuries: breath transcends mere oxygen exchange—it embodies divine intentionality, bridging our physical form to heightened states of consciousness and divine presence. The ancients recognized breath as sacred; now science is revealing why.

THE SACRED VALUE OF MENTAL STILLNESS

When your mind wanders during times of quiet—what many would call "boredom"—your brain's "default mode network" activates. This neural pathway, composed of interconnected regions including the medial prefrontal cortex, posterior cingulate cortex, and temporal parietal junction, isn't a distraction from spiritual growth but rather a gateway to deeper contemplation. Neuroscientists have discovered that this network consumes up to twenty percent of the body's energy despite being active during "rest," highlighting its fundamental importance to our cognitive functioning. It's in these quiet spaces that our most profound questions surface: about purpose, meaning, our relationship with God, and our place in His creation. This describes some of the root causes behind the mental health crisis of so many of our youth today.

In our modern world, we've developed an aversion to these quiet moments. We fill every second with stimulation—scrolling through social media, jumping between notifications, consuming endless content. This constant activity engages our brain's task-positive networks while suppressing the default mode network. Neuroimaging studies show that persistent digital stimulation can actually reshape neural pathways, making it increasingly difficult to access the contemplative state. This continuous external focus prevents us from entering the mental state where deep spiritual insight occurs and where crucial integration of our experiences takes place.

LIVING FROM THE SPIRIT: MOVING IN ASCENDED PERCEPTION

The Holy Spirit is our guide into revelation. Jesus promised, "When the Spirit of Truth comes, He will guide you into all truth... He will tell you what is yet to come" (John 16:13, NIV). Living an ascended life means abiding in this constant unfolding of divine wisdom.

As Bill Johnson describes it, abiding is "the continuous awareness of the presence of the Holy Spirit upon our lives" (*The Supernatural Power of a Transformed Mind*, 2005, p. 42). It's not a mental effort but a surrender to the Spirit's leading. Just as a branch naturally bears fruit by remaining connected to the vine (John 15:5), we bear the fruit of revelation when we remain in awareness of our union with Him.

When we yield to the Spirit's guidance, revelation becomes our daily reality. The "perceived" veil between Heaven and earth grows thinner as we embrace our co-seated position with Christ (Ephesians 2:6, NKJV). We're not striving for revelation—we're awakening to the reality that we already have access to Heaven's perspective.

ZŌĒ: LIVING FROM THE DIVINE LIFE OF GOD

For much of my Christian walk, I thought of eternal life as something that started after I died. It was a future reward, a distant promise. But understanding *zōē* shattered that illusion. *Zōē* isn't just biological life—it's the uncreated, divine life of God Himself, infused into us here and now.

"I have come that you may have life (*zōē*), life in superabundance!" — John 10:10 (TPT)

🔥 *Zōē* is not something we wait for—it is something we live from.

🔥 *Zōē* is not about surviving—it is about overflowing.

🔥 *Zōē* is not a distant hope—it is our present reality.

"Faith is not a decision; faith is the most amazing discovery! The love of God realized awakens belief! Faith is not blind, neither is it unconscious; faith knows." — *Divine Embrace* by Francois Du Toit

"God believes that we are fully represented in Christ, which takes circumcision or any contribution of the flesh out of the equation. Love fuels belief and sets faith in motion. It is easy for love to believe." — Galatians 5:6, Mirror Study Bible by Francois du Toit

These profound insights reveal a transformational truth that has been obscured through mistranslation in many Bible versions. Galatians 2:20, KJV, TPT in its original language states, "I live by the faith OF the Son of God, who loved me and gave Himself for me." Many translations render this as faith "in" the Son of God, but the original text clearly indicates it is the very faith OF Christ operating through us.

This distinction is revolutionary and immensely freeing! We don't need to generate faith through our own effort or "muster up enough faith" as if it were a work of our flesh. Rather, we simply awaken to and live from the faith that God has already placed within us. It is His love that awakens His faith within us. When we truly experience the revelation of how much He loves us, His faith naturally begins to operate through us.

I had spent years praying for God's presence, crying out for more of Him, not realizing that His very life was already infused into me. *Zōē* means I am not separate from God's power—I am a carrier of it. The moment I stopped seeing myself as an empty vessel waiting to be filled and started recognizing that I was already full of His life, everything changed. I am designed for outpouring!

🔥 I stopped praying from lack—I started declaring from fullness.

🔥 I stopped asking for God's power—I started living from His indwelling presence.

🔥 I stopped fearing death—I started realizing I had already been resurrected into divine life.

"Christ in you, the hope of glory!" —Colossians 1:27 (TPT)

KENN GILL: THE HITCHING ANALOGY

My spiritual father, Kenn Gill, often describes the Spirit-engaged life as being completely hitched to God, like a trailer securely connected to a powerful vehicle. The trailer has no independent movement of its own— it follows wherever the vehicle goes, without resistance or striving.

Kenn explains that when the trailer is hitched, the safety chains are locked, and everything is secure. It doesn't need to push forward on its own—the power of the vehicle determines its movement. In the same way, when we yield to the Holy Spirit, we move in alignment with God's momentum, effortlessly advancing His Kingdom.

This is the ease of ascended living. As we surrender, divine revelation flows effortlessly—not by striving but by remaining in Him.

? Wonder Questions:

? What if you've been trying to push forward in your own strength when all God wants is for you to be securely hitched to His power?

? How might your journey look different if you simply surrendered to His momentum?

THEOSIS: AWAKENING TO OUR TRUE ORIGIN

Revelation leads us into what the early Church Fathers called "theosis"—the journey of union with God. This isn't about becoming something we're not; it's awakening to what has always been true. As we step into this divine reality, we realize that our existence isn't merely the product of creation, but an eternal "uncreated" reality in Christ before time began.

This profound truth, deeply explored by Maximus the Confessor, unveils that our origin isn't limited to time and space but is anchored in the Lamb slain before the foundation of the world (Revelation 13:8, NKJV). Maximus taught that the Incarnation wasn't simply a reaction to the Fall but God's eternal purpose from before creation itself (Various Texts on Theology, 1.13, 7th century). Christ didn't come merely to fix what was broken—He is the blueprint, the archetype, the divine Logos in whom all things have always existed (Colossians 1:16-17).

The Incarnation wasn't Plan B; it was always Plan A—the eternal merging of divinity and humanity, the perfect expression of God's love in time and beyond time. To wake up to theosis is to realize that we aren't merely created beings trying to reach God—we are expressions of His eternal life, invited into participation with His divine nature (2 Peter 1:4, NKJV).

Many of the early church fathers understood that we are in Christ, and were never truly separate from Him. We were never outside of God's presence, never distant from our true home in Him. The cross and resurrection didn't merely reconcile us to God—they revealed that we were always in Him, hidden in divine reality before the world began (Ephesians 1:4).

🔥 Theosis is the great awakening—the realization that we were never merely created, but eternally found in Him.

JESUS: THE BRIDGE BETWEEN AIN SOPH AUR AND OUR ASCENSION

Jesus, the radiant expression of the Father (Hebrews 1:3), is the bridge or door between Ain Soph Aur (Endless Light) and our earthly experience. To live in revelation is to live in oneness with Christ, where all things hidden become known, and we move as He moves, fully aligned with the rhythms of Heaven.

As we engage in ascension, we too step into divine perception—moving beyond earthly reasoning into the limitless wisdom of God. This isn't about striving but about recognizing where we already are: co-seated with Christ in heavenly places (Ephesians 2:6, NKJV).

Gregory of Nyssa, one of the early Church Fathers, described this process as "eternal progress in the infinite"—a continuous ascension into ever-increasing glory (*Life of Moses*, 2.239, 4th century). We're not climbing toward God; we're awakening to greater awareness of our union with Him that has always existed. The more we "see" from this position of oneness, the more revelation naturally flows through us.

TESTIMONIES: LIVING OUT REVELATION IN DAILY LIFE

Chantal: Visions of Our Heavenly Position

Years ago, I had a dream where I saw Flō positioned at the top of a massive corporate building that extended into the clouds and beyond, representing our place in the Heavenly realm. This vision resonated deeply with an ascension experience Bryan had during a recent prayer meeting where he saw himself with his head in the heavens and his body rooted on earth—a vivid picture of our bi-locational nature in Christ.

We are called to operate from this higher perspective, setting our minds on things above (Colossians 3:2), and serving as conduits of Heaven's reality to earth. This heavenly positioning applies not only to our personal lives but to all that we steward—including Flō. We are called to make "on earth as it is in heaven" our new normal.

Bryan: Roaring in the Spirit Over My Daughter

There was a moment of deep intercession for my daughter, Bryn, that I will never forget. She was going through a challenging season, and as our prayer team gathered, I sat next to her on the couch, my arm around her. What began as a typical prayer quickly moved beyond words—my spirit felt like it expanded, engulfing her with a deep sense of love and protection.

Suddenly, I sensed a roar rising within me, like a lion roaring over her with divine authority. This wasn't just a father's prayer; it was the Spirit of God roaring through me and with me, declaring a breakthrough over her life without a sound in the natural realm.

This moment was a tangible expression of Romans 8:26, where the Holy Spirit within me prayed with groans too deep for words, in perfect alignment with God's will for Bryn. We witnessed a profound breakthrough that day, both in prayer and in her life. It reminded me that when we surrender to the Spirit, allowing Him to intercede through us, His power is released, and His perfect will is accomplished.

REVELATION THROUGH CONTEMPLATION

Justin Paul Abraham teaches about accessing revelation through what he calls "contemplative ascension"—a practice of quieting the mind and entering into the presence of God with childlike wonder (*Beyond Human*, 2017, p. 112). This approach opens us to receive divine insight not through mental striving but through restful awareness.

In my experience, some of the most profound revelations have come during times of silent communion with God. When I step away from the noise and busyness of life to simply be with Him, my spirit becomes attuned to His voice. It's in these moments of quiet contemplation that Heaven's perspective often breaks through with crystal clarity.

Liz Wright describes this as "dwelling in the secret place," where we receive not just information but transformation (*Dancing in the Glory*, 2016, p. 64). As we spend time in God's presence without agenda or demand, our spiritual senses are awakened to perceive what He is revealing. This isn't about passivity but about active receptivity—positioning ourselves to receive what Heaven wants to unveil.

"Be still, and know that I am God."—Psalm 46:10 (NIV)

"Silence is God's first language; everything else is a poor translation." —Thomas Keating, *Invitation to Love: The Way of Christian Contemplation*

Keating's profound insight reminds us that in our quest to ascend and experience heavenly realities, sometimes the most powerful gateway is not found in more words or greater effort, but in the sacred silence where our spirits naturally align with Heaven's frequency.

Ascension is beautifully interwoven with the gentle, quiet posture of contemplative prayer. Unlike prayer as we often understand it—filled with speaking, requesting, and seeking—contemplative prayer invites us into the profound simplicity of silence and stillness before God. This practice isn't about reaching for spiritual experiences or ascending through our efforts. Instead, it's about recognizing and resting in the reality that we are already seated with Christ in heavenly places (Ephesians 2:6, NKJV).

FROM REVELATION TO MANIFESTATION

Revelation is never meant to remain as mere knowledge. Its purpose is manifestation—bringing Heaven's realities into tangible expression on earth. As we receive divine insight, we become responsible for stewarding it into reality through our faith, declarations, and actions.

Bill Johnson often says, "We're not just looking for visitation; we're looking for habitation" (*Hosting the Presence*, 2012, p. 35). We are awakening to oneness and the illusion of separation. This means revelation should lead to permanent changes in how we live, not just momentary spiritual experiences. When God reveals something to us, it's an invitation to partner with Him in making it visible to others.

This process of manifestation often follows a pattern:

1. *Revelation*—Receiving heavenly insight

2. *Declaration*—Speaking it forth in the faith of Jesus

3. *Demonstration*—Acting in alignment with what was revealed

4. *Transformation*—Witnessing reality shift to reflect Heaven's truth

Think of it like an architect receiving a blueprint. The blueprint alone doesn't construct the building—it must be declared (communicated to the team), demonstrated (built according to the design), and ultimately transformed from concept to reality. Similarly, heavenly revelation requires our active partnership to become manifest on earth.

THE INVITATION TO LIVE AS SONS OF LIGHT

We have the might of Christ. Revelation isn't something we attain—it's something we awaken to. We're invited to step into divine wisdom, moving beyond earthly reasoning and into the supernatural light of Christ. The more we live from this place, the more we see from above and release Heaven's realities into the earth.

As Dallas Willard taught, spiritual life isn't about acquiring more information, but about transformation—becoming the kind of person who naturally lives from Heaven's perspective (*Renovation of the Heart*, 2002, p. 14). This transformation happens as we practice living in the awareness that we are already citizens of Heaven, with full access to its wisdom and resources.

"This letter is from Simeon Peter, a loving servant and an apostle of Jesus Christ. I am writing to those who have been given a faith as equally precious as ours through the righteousness of our God and Savior, Jesus Christ." —2 Peter 1:1 (TPT)

The footnotes from TPT tell us that even our faith has been given to us by a loving Father!

Grace overwhelms us when we realize that faith rests not on our ability but upon the finished work of Jesus. We don't strive to earn it—we awaken to it.

PRACTICAL STEPS TO CULTIVATING REVELATION

Here are some practical ways to cultivate a lifestyle of divine revelation:

- *Morning Posturing*—Begin each day by consciously setting your mind on things above. Declare your position in Christ and invite the Holy Spirit to guide your thoughts and perceptions.

- *Sacred Pauses*—Throughout your day, take brief moments to pause, breathe, and realign with Heaven's perspective. These micro-ascensions help maintain spiritual awareness.

- *Scripture Meditation*—Spend time dwelling on God's Word not just for information but for transformation. Ask the Holy Spirit to reveal the living reality behind the written text.

- *Journaling*—Record impressions, dreams, and insights you receive. This practice helps you recognize patterns of revelation over time.

- *Community Confirmation*—Share what you're receiving with trusted spiritual companions who can help confirm and refine your understanding.

- *Obedient Response*—Put revelation into practice quickly. Immediate obedience opens the door to greater revelation.

- *Gratitude Practice*—Regularly thank God for the revelation He's given, acknowledging your dependence on His insight rather than your own understanding.

APPLICATION ACTIVATIONS

Ascension Activation: Divine Sight

Purpose: To see situations from heaven's perspective

Time Required: 10-15 minutes

Steps:

1. Find a quiet place and ask the Holy Spirit to take you into a deeper revelation of your seated position in Christ (Ephesians 2:6, NKJV).

2. Close your eyes and picture yourself seated next to Jesus in heavenly places.

3. Ask Him: "What do You see that I am not seeing?"

4. Write down any visions, thoughts, or impressions He gives you and reflect on how they can shape your life.

Expected Outcome: A fresh perspective on your circumstances that aligns with Heaven's reality rather than earthly limitations.

🔥 Spiritual Hitching Activation: Yielding to God's Momentum

Purpose: To surrender personal striving and align with divine flow

Time Required: 5-10 minutes

Steps:

1. Ask the Holy Spirit to reveal any areas where you are trying to move forward in your own strength.

2. Picture yourself as a trailer being hitched to a powerful vehicle.

3. Declare aloud: "Lord, I surrender control. I am securely hitched to Your divine flow, moving in alignment with Your power."

4. Pay attention to any shifts in your spirit as you yield to Him.

Expected Outcome: A tangible sense of release from pressure and a newfound ease in moving with God's timing.

🦁 Roaring Activation: Interceding with Kingdom Authority

Purpose: To release powerful spiritual declarations over areas needing breakthrough

Time Required: 10-15 minutes

Steps:

1. Recall an area where someone you love needs breakthrough.

2. Instead of speaking words, allow your spirit to intercede beyond language—whether through deep groanings (Romans 8:26) or even a silent roar of authority over the situation. Simply hold the person in your heart in love and rest.

3. Picture God's divine power flowing through you, your spirit expanding and covering them in love, protection, and transformation.

4. Journal the experience and watch for how breakthrough manifests in the days to come.

Expected Outcome: A supernatural release of Kingdom authority and the manifestation of breakthrough in the situation.

PURSUING CONTINUOUS REVELATION

Living in revelation isn't a one-time event but a lifestyle of continuous awareness and discovery. As we practice the presence of God and maintain our heavenly perspective, we'll find that revelation becomes increasingly natural—a constant flow rather than occasional flashes of insight.

The more we align with Heaven's frequency, the clearer its broadcast becomes. This alignment doesn't require special techniques or spiritual gymnastics; it simply requires consistent surrender and childlike faith. As Jesus taught, the Kingdom belongs to those who receive it like little children—with wonder, trust, and openness.

? Wonder Questions:

? What if the stream of divine revelation is already flowing all around you, and you only need to tune your awareness to perceive it?

? What revelations might God be eager to share with you right now?

? Will you accept the invitation to live in this continuous stream of divine revelation?

? Will you allow Heaven's perspective to transform how you see yourself, others, and the world around you?

The veil has been torn; access has been granted.

The only question that remains is: *Will you live from this place of revelation?*

☺ Reflection Questions:

? How does your perception of daily life change when you set your mind on things above (Colossians 3:1–3)?

? What practical steps can you take to shift your awareness from earthly limitations to a heavenly perspective?

? Are there areas in your life where you are striving instead of being "hitched" to God's divine movement?

? How can you surrender more deeply and allow the Holy Spirit to guide you effortlessly?

? What revelation has the Holy Spirit been stirring in your heart that you have yet to fully embrace?

? How can you position yourself to walk in greater alignment with God's divine reality?

? How might you recognize and respond to divine patterns in your daily life?

? What "coincidences" might actually be God's fingerprints?

BONUS: THIS IS THAT: DIVINE PATTERN RECOGNITION IN THE ASCENDED LIFE

WARNING: This Bonus Chapter May Cause Spontaneous "Aha!" Moments

Have you ever watched a child complete a connect-the-dots puzzle? At first, they see only scattered points on a page. But as they draw the lines between them, something magical happens—a recognizable picture emerges from what seemed random. Living the ascended life is remarkably similar—Heaven invites us to connect divine dots across our experiences, revealing the beautiful picture God has been drawing all along.

THE PROPHETIC POWER OF "THIS IS THAT"

Have you ever experienced a moment of stunning clarity when something God revealed to you in the past suddenly manifests in the present? That electrifying moment of recognition when you and your spiritual companions exchange knowing glances and declare with certainty: "This is that!"—a phrase that Chantal would joyfully declare each time the connection was made!

I call this phenomenon "divine pattern recognition," and it's one of the most thrilling aspects of living the ascended life. It's that moment when Heaven's blueprint, previously glimpsed through dreams, visions, or prophetic words, suddenly materializes in your earthly experience.

What we focus on expands. As we keep our focus on Jesus, the author and finisher of our faith (Hebrews 12:2, NIV), we can walk through any trial victoriously.

RECOGNIZING HEAVEN'S PATTERNS

Divine pattern recognition isn't about becoming detached from reality— it's about seeing reality as it truly is: infused with God's presence and purpose. As Nancy Cohen teaches in Seeing Through Heaven's Eyes (2019, 78), it is "seeing through Heaven's lens," where ordinary events become filled with prophetic significance. Through this heavenly perspective, we begin to perceive:

> God's fingerprints in seeming "coincidences" ⸭ His voice in thoughts that appear random ⸭ His guidance in apparently mundane decisions ⸭ His timing in life's unexpected turns

This supernatural discernment develops as we practice ascension-living from our seated position with Christ in heavenly places. When we engage with heavenly realities, our spiritual senses become increasingly attuned to recognize divine patterns unfolding in our everyday lives.

REAL "THIS IS THAT" MOMENTS FROM MY JOURNEY

The Beach Encounter: Divine Confirmation

Last week, during our weekly ascension time with the prayer team, I had a profound encounter with Jesus. As I began walking with Him in the spirit, I was physically sitting on a beach on the east coast of Canada with strong winds blowing and waves crashing loudly. The natural distractions were overwhelming at first. However, as I settled into the Spirit, everything shifted.

Suddenly, I saw Jesus' face in the waves, and He spoke to me, saying, "I'm in the waves, in the breeze, because I hold all things together." In that moment, the truth of Colossians 1:17, "He is before all things, and in Him all things hold together" (NIV), came alive in a new way. I realized how deeply our union with Christ connects us with everything—even the natural world. It was a reminder of Psalm 24:1, "The earth is the Lord's, and everything in it" (NIV).

This experience echoes what Celtic Christians called "thin places"—locations where the barrier between Heaven and earth seems especially transparent. St. Columba of Iona (521-597 AD) taught that creation itself reveals the Creator: "If you want to know the Creator, look at what He has created" (*Life of Columba*, Book III). Similarly, Hildegard of Bingen (1098-1179 AD) wrote of seeing divine presence in nature: "The high and the low all meet in God. The flame of the Spirit lives in all created things" (*Scivias*, Book I, Vision 3).

As often happens during ascension, Jesus took me into the cosmos—a reflection of my deep fascination with space. (God is so kind to meet us where we are and connect with us uniquely!) The wind continued to intensify around me, and in the supernatural realm, I felt like an eagle soaring on the winds of God, just as Isaiah 40:31 says, "They will soar on wings like eagles" (NIV).

As I flew, I saw various parts of the earth, as though I were observing from above, moving over a map. Suddenly, I heard the line, "Time keeps on slipping, slipping, slipping into the future," from "Fly Like an Eagle" by Steve Miller—a song I hadn't thought of in decades. It resonated deeply in my spirit, and I sensed God highlighting the significance of time, reminding me of Ecclesiastes 3:1: "There is a time for everything, and a season for every activity under the heavens" (NIV).

Divine Confirmation: When Heaven Speaks the Same Message

After the fifteen-minute ascension, I shared my experience with the team. Chantal was visibly excited as she explained that during her own ascension, she had been handed a box. Inside was a large clock, and she heard the words, "It's time." The theme of time was clearly being revealed to us by the Lord.

As we later reflected on the lyrics of the Steve Miller song, the message became even more profound: "I want to fly like an eagle... to the sea... let my spirit carry me... 'til I'm free." The song speaks of feeding the hungry, clothing the children, and housing the homeless—echoing Matthew 25:35-36, where Jesus calls us to care for those in need. The image of flying, carried by the Spirit, confirmed that what I experienced was not only real but deeply meaningful. God loves to give us encouragement.

This principle of confirmation through multiple witnesses has biblical roots. As Deuteronomy 19:15 states, "A matter must be established by the testimony of two or three witnesses" (NIV). The early church relied heavily on this principle of discernment through confirmation. Gregory the Great (540-604 AD) wrote, "When multiple souls receive the same divine impression independently, we can trust it as from God, for the Holy Spirit does not contradict Himself" (*Pastoral Rule*, Part III, Chapter 39).

As we continued discerning what the Lord was showing us individually and as a team, it became clear that God was redeeming time in this season. We were reminded that He exists outside of time (2 Peter 3:8, NIV), and His promises are being fulfilled in the "now." One of the team members shared a vision of "rich time" being possessed, revealing that while decay and death need time to operate, the realm of the Spirit exists beyond time and space.

This truth reminded us that in Christ, we are not bound by time's limitations, for He is the "Alpha and the Omega, the beginning and the end" (Revelation 22:13, NIV). We are living in a season where God's promises are coming to fruition, and our call is to step into His timing and act with Kingdom purpose.

? Wonder Questions:

? How might God be inviting you to step out of earthly time constraints and into the eternal "now" of His Kingdom?

? What promises have you been waiting for that He might be saying are available right now?

The Warehouse Vision: Dreams Becoming Reality

Another powerful "this is that" moment came through a prophetic dream Chantal had years ago. In this dream, she saw our company, Flō, operating out of a warehouse facility—something completely outside our business model at the time.

When she shared this vision with me, I responded with logical skepticism: "That's interesting, but warehousing isn't part of our business model." As an engineer, I naturally assessed the dream against our current operational framework rather than seeing it as a glimpse into future possibilities.

Fast forward to 2025, and we found ourselves opening the Flō Assurance Centre—located in a large warehouse exactly as Chantal had seen in her dream years earlier. What once seemed disconnected from our business reality had manifested precisely as she had envisioned.

This experience reinforced an important truth about divine pattern recognition: God often reveals aspects of our future that don't make sense within our current understanding or business models. What appears impossible or irrelevant in one season becomes the exact path forward in another.

The warehouse vision reminds us to hold prophetic insights with reverence even when they don't align with our present reality. Heaven's blueprints often arrive years before their earthly manifestation, requiring patient stewardship until the appointed time of fulfillment.

The Mountain Climbing Vision: Conference Confirmation

Once, we were asked to lead a conference breakout session on "Ruling and Reigning with Christ" at the Kingdom Builders Forum. During the session, as we began talking about the Holy Spirit, I sensed the Holy Spirit prompting us to delve into deeper spiritual matters. This naturally led us to discuss Ascension.

One attendee asked if we could engage in Ascension right then, and Chantal and I agreed. As soon as the Ascension process began, I saw a vision of an angel standing beside her, dressed in mountain climbing gear—a curious sight that initially didn't make much sense to me.

However, the vision continued to unfold, showing Mount Zion and many angels with climbing equipment, passing ropes down to the people in the room. As people ascended, aided by the angels, they reached a part of the mountain covered in beautiful white snow and began "slaloming" up the hill on skis.

I hesitated to share my vision of the angel in mountain climbing gear standing beside Chantal, as it seemed so unusual, but when I did, Chantal immediately recognized it from a dream she had in 2022. In that dream, I had given her orange and purple mountain climbing gear, symbolizing preparation for entering the realm of Ascension.

This moment at the conference became a public manifestation of that vision, as God was clearly inviting His people to ascend to heavenly places, co-seated with Christ. It was a powerful "this is that" moment for everyone present. We will share more on this in the final chapter.

LEARNING THE LANGUAGE OF HEAVEN

As we grow in ascension, we begin to recognize divine patterns more readily. It's like learning to read music—what once appeared as random dots and lines on a page gradually transforms into a beautiful symphony as your understanding deepens.

The Holy Spirit trains our spiritual senses to:

◆ Perceive connections between past revelations and present circumstances ◆ Recognize divine timing when prophecies align with current events ◆ Discern the spiritual significance behind natural occurrences ◆ Track the consistent threads of God's purposes through seemingly unrelated experiences

This skill develops through practice. As you engage more consistently with heavenly realms, you'll find yourself exclaiming "this is that!" with increasing frequency.

✦ ASCENSION ACTIVATION: DIVINE PATTERN RECOGNITION ✦

Ready to develop your own divine pattern recognition? Here are practical steps I recommend:

1. Keep a revelation journal—Record dreams, visions, prophetic words, and spiritual impressions you receive. Date each entry.

2. Practice regular ascension—Set aside time daily to shift your consciousness to heavenly realities, becoming more aware of your seated position with Christ.

3. Create review rhythms—Schedule regular times (weekly/ monthly) to look back through your journal, asking the Holy Spirit to highlight connections.

4. Share with trusted companions—Divine patterns often become clearer when verbalized and confirmed in community.

5. Declare "This is that!"—When you recognize a pattern or fulfillment, boldly declare it, anchoring the revelation in your conscious awareness.

Remember that divine pattern recognition isn't about predicting the future—it's about recognizing God's orchestration as it unfolds. It's seeing His hand weaving the tapestry of your life and the world around you with perfect precision.

THE JOY OF RECOGNITION

There's something uniquely thrilling about those "this is that" moments. They validate our spiritual experiences, confirm God's intimate involvement in our lives, and strengthen our faith in His perfect timing.

When you and your spiritual companions exchange those knowing glances and declare "this is that," you're participating in a sacred reality that transcends time—a reality where Heaven's blueprints manifest on Earth through awakened sons and daughters.

Ephesians 4:16 reminds us beautifully of how interconnected we are, intricately "knitted and joined together," with supernatural growth flowing directly from God (NIV). This profound truth is at the heart of our divine cluster—each of us uniquely gifted and essential, yet exponentially more powerful when connected. And as we recognize and embrace this interconnectedness, we experience a "FLŌ"—a divine momentum propelling us collectively higher and further. Truly, we need each other to fully ascend into the greater realms that God has prepared for us.

This divine pattern recognition isn't reserved for spiritual elites. It's available to everyone willing to ascend, to shift their consciousness from earthly limitations to heavenly perspectives, and to train their spiritual senses through regular engagement with God's presence.

? Wonder Question:

? What dream, vision, or prophetic word from your past might be finding its "this is that" moment in your present?

The veil between Heaven and Earth has been torn. As you learn to see with Heaven's eyes, you'll discover that life is filled with "this is that" moments—divine connections and fulfillments that have been there all along, waiting for you to recognize them.

Think of divine pattern recognition like putting on spiritual 3D glasses—suddenly, what was flat and ordinary jumps into vivid, multi-dimensional reality. The scenes haven't changed, but your ability to perceive their depth has been transformed. As you practice seeing with Heaven's eyes, these moments of recognition will become more frequent and more thrilling, like treasure hunters who have discovered the secret map to hidden riches that were there all along.

The journey of ascension is an invitation to see—truly see—the divine orchestration that surrounds you every day. As you recognize these patterns, you'll find yourself living increasingly from Heaven's perspective, partnering with God to bring His Kingdom realities into every aspect of your life.

This is that. And it's just the beginning.

CHAPTER 5: ✦🔥 CROSSING OVER- THE JOURNEY FROM THE FAMILIAR TO THE DIVINE

🚨 WARNING: This Chapter May Cause Unexpected Border Crossings 🚨

Proceed with passport in hand (and comfort zone left behind)!

Potential side effects include: ✅ Finding yourself thinking like a heavenly citizen instead of an earthly resident ✅ Spontaneously seeing divine solutions to mundane problems ✅ Developing an addiction to supernatural perspective ✅ No longer fitting comfortably in boxes labeled "normal"

Have you ever watched a child learning to swim? They cling to the edge of the pool, knuckles white, eyes wide—absolutely certain that letting go means certain doom. Then that magical moment comes when they finally release their grip and discover they've been designed to float all along. Crossing over into God's supernatural realities feels a lot like that—terrifying until you realize you were made for this all along.

What if the greatest adventures in God begin the moment we step beyond what we can see?

The word Hebrew means "to cross over," and Abraham is considered the first Hebrew because he was the first to cross over by faith. Called out of Ur of the Chaldeans, Abram obeyed God's voice, leaving his homeland and stepping into an eternal covenant (Genesis 12:1-3). This act of faith became the inception point of the Hebrews, as Scripture declares, "Abraham believed God, and it was credited to him as righteousness" (Genesis 15:6, NIV).

Throughout Scripture, we see this pattern repeated: God calls His people to cross over from one reality into another, from the familiar into the unknown, from the visible into the invisible realm. This crossing over isn't just a historical theme—it's a spiritual principle that defines our journey of ascension.

THE PATTERN OF CROSSING OVER

Abraham's journey wasn't just a personal calling but the foundation of a people chosen by God to carry His promises. Renamed from Abram to Abraham ("father of many nations"), he became the spiritual father of all who live by faith (Romans 4:16-17, NIV).

From Abraham came Isaac, the child of promise, and from Isaac came Jacob. In a pivotal moment, Jacob wrestled with God and was renamed Israel, meaning "One who struggles with God" or "God prevails" (Genesis 32:28, NIV). His twelve sons formed the structural foundation of God's covenant people.

Faith is the thread woven through this lineage. Abraham's obedience to cross over set the pattern for all who would follow God by faith, ultimately foreshadowing Jesus Christ, the Lion of Judah, in whom God's promise to Abraham—that all nations would be blessed through his seed (Genesis 22:18, NIV)—was fulfilled.

? **Wonder Question:**

? Where in your life is God calling you to "cross over" from the familiar into a new realm of faith and promise?

OUR SPIRITUAL INHERITANCE: CROSSING OVER INTO HEAVENLY REALMS

The book of Hebrews calls us to step into a deeper dimension of faith and spiritual understanding. True to the meaning of the word Hebrews—"those who crossed over"—this is more than a historical identity; it is a spiritual invitation to journey:

- From darkness to light
- From doubt to faith
- From earthly limitations to heavenly realities

Through Christ, believers are invited to live in the fullness of their identity, not confined by what is seen but rooted in the eternal truths of Heaven.

"Just as Abraham crossed over by faith into God's promises, we too are called to live boldly in the faith that enables us to draw on heavenly resources and fulfill our earthly calling."

Hebrews 3:14-15 speaks of our part in this transformative process: "For we are mingled with the Messiah, if we will continue unshaken in this confident assurance from the beginning until the end. For again, the Scriptures say, 'If only today you would listen to his voice. Don't make him angry by hardening your hearts, as you did in the wilderness rebellion.'" (TPT)

THE GREAT REVERSAL: GOD HAS ALREADY CROSSED OVER TO US

The deepest truth is that we're not crossing over to reach God—we're awakening to the reality that God has already crossed over to us. In Christ, the divine and human have been forever united. Our journey isn't about trying to get somewhere we're not; it's about recognizing where we've always been in Him.

This truth transforms our understanding of faith from striving to seeing. As Gregory of Nyssa taught, "We don't achieve union with God—we awaken to it" (*On the Soul and the Resurrection*, 4th century).

TRAINING OUR SPIRITUAL SENSES

The concept of spiritual perception may seem abstract to modern readers, but it's thoroughly biblical and has been embraced by Christians throughout history. When the author of Hebrews speaks of those who have "their powers of discernment trained by constant practice to distinguish good from evil" (Hebrews 5:14, ESV), he's using language that parallels how we develop our physical senses. Jonathan Edwards, the renowned 18th-century theologian and leader of the Great Awakening, wrote extensively about what he called "spiritual sensation"—the God-given capacity to perceive divine realities. Similarly, C.S. Lewis described Heaven as a place of "more seeing, not less; more taste, not less." What we're exploring isn't new or speculative, but rather the recovery of biblical truth.

The Bible frequently uses sensory language to describe our relationship with God: we "taste and see that the Lord is good" (Psalm 34:8, NKJV), we're called to have "ears to hear" spiritual truths (Matthew 11:1, NKJV), and Paul prays for "the eyes of your heart" to be enlightened (Ephesians 1:18, NIV). While Scripture doesn't explicitly outline five spiritual senses directly mirroring our physical ones, this metaphorical language helps us understand how we perceive and interact with God's presence.

Through intentional practice and yielding to the Holy Spirit, our spiritual discernment becomes increasingly sharpened, enabling us to recognize God's voice and engage with heavenly realities. As we grow in discerning spiritual truths, we become more equipped to live in the reality of the Kingdom. This isn't mysticism—it's the normal Christian life Jesus modeled, where we perceive and respond to the activity of Heaven around us.

ASCENSION ACTIVATION: SPIRITUAL SENSES

1. Find a quiet place where you won't be disturbed for 5-10 minutes

2. Close your eyes and take three deep breaths to center yourself

3. Ask the Holy Spirit: "Would You heighten my awareness of Heaven's reality around me?"

4. Remain in a posture of receptivity, not striving

5. Notice what impressions come—perhaps a sense of peace, a flash of light, a subtle sound, or a feeling of God's presence

6. Don't analyze or question what comes; simply receive

7. Afterward, journal what you experienced, even if it seemed small or subtle

MOVING TOWARD SPIRITUAL MATURITY

Hebrews 6:1 invites believers to "progress toward spiritual maturity, advancing into perfection" (TPT). This isn't a call to striving or self-effort, but rather an invitation to awaken to deeper dimensions of what is already true in Christ.

Spiritual maturity isn't something we achieve through religious performance; it's a progressive unveiling of the limitless reality we already possess in Jesus. As we grow, we're simply becoming more aware of who we already are and what we already have in Him. It's like a flower naturally unfolding—not through effort, but through the grace-filled process of receiving light and nourishment.

This growth happens as we receive revelation of God's tremendous love for us. Each new awakening draws us deeper into the limitless faith of God, opening realms of discovery that have always existed but are now being perceived with increasing clarity.

Hebrews 10:19 (NKJV) encourages us to "live beyond the sacred threshold," reminding us that through Christ, we're already invited past the outer courts into the Holy of Holies—into intimate relationship with God Himself. This isn't something we earn; it's our birthright as His children that we're awakening to.

When Jesus declared, "It is finished," He was not merely concluding His mission but inaugurating a new reality available to all. In this finished work, we discover:

⁌ Forgiveness that's already complete—not something we work toward

⁌ Restored oneness with God—not a distant goal but a present reality

⁌ Freedom from sin—not a battle we must win but a victory already secured

⁌ A new identity as God's beloved children—not an achievement but a gift to be recognized

The process of spiritual maturity is simply growing in our awareness of these truths. As theologian Karl Barth beautifully expressed, "In Jesus

Christ, God has reconciled the world to himself. We don't make this true by believing it. It is true, and therefore we believe it."

Our journey isn't about becoming something new but awakening to what has always been true since Christ's resurrection. He tore the veil of the illusion of separation and secured our eternal victory. Every step forward is actually a step deeper into the reality that already exists in Him.

THE ZION-REALM: OUR PRESENT REALITY

Hebrews paints a powerful picture of our spiritual reality, reminding us that we have already entered into the "Zion-realm," the city of the Living God, the New Jerusalem.

"By contrast, we have already come near to God in a totally different realm, the Zion-realm, for we have entered the city of the Living God, which is the New Jerusalem in Heaven! We have joined the festal gathering of myriads of angels in their joyous celebration!" —Hebrews 12:22 (TPT)

Notice the phrase "already come"—this isn't future tense. Through Christ, we have already crossed over into heavenly realities. Through Christ, we have been given access to heavenly realities, which we grow in our ability to experience and manifest. As new creations, united with Him, we carry the limitless power and presence of His Kingdom into every aspect of our lives.

This crossing over is not just a one-time event but a continuous journey of living in union with Christ. It challenges us to rise above earthly distractions and focus on eternal realities, walking as citizens of Heaven while transforming the world around us.

? **Wonder Question:**

? How is God calling you to "cross over" into the deeper realms of faith and engage the limitless possibilities of His power and love?

OUR KING-PRIEST IDENTITY

Hebrews 7 introduces us to Melchizedek, a king-priest whose order predates the Levitical priesthood. Verse 16 says, "[Melchizedek] became a priest, not by meeting the old requirements of belonging to the tribe of Levi, but through the power of an indestructible life" (TPT). This points to the resurrection life we now have in Christ—a life that is eternal and powerful, enabling us to reign as priests forever.

Hebrews 7:17 reiterates that "You are a priest forever in the order of Melchizedek" (TPT), speaking to the eternal priesthood that we share with Christ. This dual identity means we function both in authority (kings) and intimacy (priests). We are called to rule in the earthly realm with heavenly authority while ministering to God in intimate worship and communion.

BOLDLY ENTERING THE HOLY OF HOLIES

Hebrews 10:19-21 invites us to boldly enter the most holy place in the heavenly realm. "And now we are brothers and sisters in God's family because of the blood of Jesus, and He welcomes us to come right into the most holy sanctuary in the heavenly realm—a new and living way for us to approach God" (TPT).

Faith is the key to accessing this unseen, heavenly realm and living from that reality here on earth. Hebrews 11:1 declares that "Now faith brings our hopes into reality and becomes the foundation needed to acquire the things we long for. It is all the evidence required to prove what is still unseen" (TPT).

Faith in this context isn't about trying harder to believe—it's about seeing more clearly what has always been true. When we see from Heaven's perspective, faith becomes the natural response to divine reality, not a struggle to believe against the evidence. Faith is a gift from God.

MAKING THE INVISIBLE KINGDOM VISIBLE: MY JOURNEY

The Bible is filled with stories of transformation—where people's understanding of God and His Kingdom expanded beyond their previous limitations. Whether it was Peter's vision on the rooftop that challenged his understanding of who could be included in God's family, or Paul's encounter on the Damascus road that completely reframed his understanding of Jesus, God delights in broadening our perspective of His Kingdom.

My own journey of discovering how to live with Heaven's perspective in everyday situations didn't begin with dramatic visions or supernatural encounters. It started with simple, practical choices to apply Kingdom principles in the most ordinary areas of my life. What I learned along the way is that the supernatural often manifests most powerfully through our willingness to be faithful in seemingly small things.

By continually aligning every area of my work with God's Kingdom values, I transitioned from seeing myself as an owner to understanding my role as a steward of God's resources. As I made decisions based on Kingdom values—such as integrity, love, generosity, and service—I saw a transformation. What was once a secular enterprise became a mission field, where God's presence is reflected in every decision.

I realized I wasn't trying to "bring" God's presence into my business—I was awakening to the reality that He was already there, waiting for me to recognize and partner with Him. The divide between sacred and secular was never real—it was just a perception I had inherited that needed to be healed.

◆ **Applying Kingdom Principles:**

❓ Where in your life or work is God inviting you to cross over from worldly patterns to Kingdom principles?

? What would it look like to steward your resources, talents, and position as belongings of the King?

? How might seeing yourself as a conduit of Heaven's reality change your approach to daily tasks and decisions?

CHIEF SPIRITUAL OFFICER: STEWARD OF KINGDOM DNA

As the CEO of Flō Energy Solutions Inc., I am first and foremost the CSO (Chief Spiritual Officer), a custodian of Kingdom DNA as positioned by God. In this role, I align our business with God's order, leading to human flourishing for everyone—believers and non-believers alike.

Prayer and spiritual alignment have become central to our business strategy. Our intention is for every decision to flow from a place of divine guidance. I believe true Kingdom success requires operating in excellence in the natural world while drawing on the power of the supernatural.

"Faith empowers us to see that the universe was created and beautifully coordinated by the power of God's words! He spoke, and the invisible realm gave birth to all that is seen." —Hebrews 11:3 (TPT)

The natural world is born from the invisible realm, and we are called to engage the invisible realm of Heaven to give birth to supernatural realities in the natural world. As Kingdom leaders, we must keep our eyes fixed on the "ultimate reward"—the lasting impact of advancing God's Kingdom.

In this way, we are gateways of Heaven to earth, bridging the natural and the supernatural, bringing God's Kingdom into full manifestation.

FINDING KINGDOM IN THE MIDST OF SUFFERING

Even in the midst of deep personal suffering, I encountered the Kingdom. Grief is a transitioning emotion—one we're meant to feel and move through. It's a necessary process of moving from the old to the new, or moving through something painful, whether loss, hurt, or suffering. But with Jesus, it's also meant to be a grace process.

After the tragic loss of my daughter, instead of being overcome by grief, I experienced the supernatural peace of God. By surrendering my pain and allowing His grace to flow through my brokenness, I found renewed purpose.

This wasn't because I mastered some spiritual technique—it was because in my darkest hour, the veil between Heaven and earth thinned, and I awakened to a reality that had always been there: God's presence had never left me. I wasn't "bringing" peace into my suffering; I was discovering the peace that had always been available. This crossing over from grief to grace wasn't about my effort but about my awareness shifting from earthly tragedy to heavenly perspective.

😌 Reflection Questions:

? As you examine your own life, are there any areas where you may be operating with a sacred-secular divide?

? How can you realign those areas to reflect the truth that all of life is sacred in the Kingdom of God?

TRANSFORMATION THROUGH TENDING THE GARDEN OF OUR HEARTS

"Your inward life is now sprouting, bringing forth fruit. What a beautiful paradise unfolds within you. When I'm near you, I smell aromas of the finest spice, for many clusters of my exquisite fruit now grow within your inner garden." —Song of Songs 4:13-15 (TPT)

We are called to tend the inner garden of our hearts, awakening to the fruit of the Spirit that already exists within us through our union with Christ. The Song of Songs beautifully portrays this garden of our true nature through poetic imagery:

◆ Love: Pomegranates of passion ◆ Joy: Henna from Heaven ◆ Peace: Spikenard ◆ Patience: Saffron ◆ Kindness: Calamus from the cross ◆ Goodness: Sacred cinnamon ◆ Faith: Scented woods ◆ Gentleness: Myrrh ◆ Strength of spirit: Aloe as eagles ascending

"We are coworkers with God, and you are His cultivated garden, the house He is building." (1 Corinthians 3:7-9 TPT). When we partner with God in tending to our spiritual garden, we're simply awakening to the supernatural growth He has already planted within us.

The beautiful paradox is that these fruits are not something we manufacture through religious effort—they've always been within us as expressions of Christ's nature. Our role isn't to produce what isn't there but to awaken to what has already been planted. As we become conscious of our union with Christ, these fruits naturally manifest through abiding, not striving.

TRANSFORMATION FROM CHILDLIKE FAITH TO HEAVENLY CITIZENSHIP

"Truly I tell you, unless you change and become like little children, you will never enter the kingdom of heaven." —Matthew 18:3 (NIV)

Childlike faith is characterized by wonder, surrender, dependence, trust, openness, and teachability—qualities that lead to true freedom in Christ.

When we surrender our lives to Jesus, we begin to awaken as citizens of Heaven on earth. Heaven itself resides within us, making us conduits of Heaven's realities on earth.

"Living within you is the Christ who floods you with the expectation of glory! This mystery of Christ, embedded within us, becomes a heavenly treasure chest of hope filled with the riches of glory for his people, and God wants everyone to know it!" —Colossians 1:27 (TPT)

This isn't about crossing over to where we've never been—it's about recognizing where we've always belonged. In Christ, we are not earning citizenship; we are awakening to it.

TRANSFORMATION TESTIMONY: CHANTAL'S EXPERIENCE

While praying for Flō, I began to ask God to release favor over the company. But the Lord stopped me, saying I needed to identify fully as one with the Flō's people and no longer see myself as separate. The Lord reminded me that when Jesus came to earth, He fully identified with us. In the same way, He called me to identify with those I was praying for, changing my language from "God, do this for them" to "God, do this for us."

When I began to fully identify with those God had planted me amongst, my prayers and work took on a new level of passion. I shifted from a mindset of separation—thinking of "me" and "them"—to a mindset of oneness with the family God was grafting me into.

"One God and Father of all, who is over all and through all and in all."
—Ephesians 4:5 (NIV)

"And to be transformed as you embrace the glorious Christ-within as your new life and live in union with Him! For God has re-created you all over again in His perfect righteousness, and you now belong to Him in the realm of true holiness... for we all belong to one another!" —Ephesians 4:24 (TPT)

This is the unity we are called to be transformed into—being one with God and one with each other.

CROSSING OVER IN DAILY LIFE: PRACTICAL APPLICATIONS

The concept of crossing over isn't just theological—it's intensely practical. Here are 5 ways to apply this principle in daily life:

1. *From Fear to Faith*: Every time we choose faith over fear, we're crossing over into the reality of God's Kingdom. When circumstances seem overwhelming, declare your citizenship in Heaven and the authority that comes with it.

2. *From Natural Thinking to Supernatural Perspective*: Train yourself to pause throughout the day and ask, "What does Heaven say about this situation?" This simple practice helps you cross over from earthly wisdom to divine insight.

3. *From Isolation to Kingdom Community*: Cross over from individualism to authentic community where heavenly realities are

experienced corporately, as Chantal discovered in her journey with Flō.

4. *From Performance to Rest*: Cross over from striving to prove your worth to resting in your identity as God's beloved. From this place of rest, true Kingdom productivity flows.

5. *From Earthly Ambition to Heavenly Purpose*: Cross over from building your own kingdom to advancing God's. Let your definition of success be determined by Heaven's values, not the world's.

These crossings aren't about working harder to reach a new state— they're about awakening to the reality that already exists, shifting our awareness from illusion to truth.

✦ ASCENSION ACTIVATION: CROSSING OVER ✦

1. Identify one area in your life where God is inviting you to cross over into new spiritual territory. It might be in your work, relationships, ministry, or personal life.

2. Write down the beliefs or patterns that have kept you on the familiar side of the river.

3. Now, write what crossing over in this area would look like and feel like. How would your thoughts, actions, and attitudes change?

4. Create a simple prayer or declaration of faith that marks your decision to cross over, and speak it aloud daily for the next twenty-one days.

5. Find someone who can hold you accountable and pray with you as you step into this new territory.

THE CONTINUOUS JOURNEY OF CROSSING OVER

Crossing over into heavenly realities isn't a one-time event—it's a continuous and limitless journey of faith. Just as the Israelites had to cross the Jordan before possessing the Promised Land, we too must continually choose to step out of what is familiar and into what God is revealing.

Remember that you are already seated with Christ in heavenly places. You have already crossed over into the Zion-realm. Now, it's about living from this truth, allowing it to transform how you think, pray, work, and relate to others.

Think of crossing over like learning to ride a bicycle—at first, it seems impossible and terrifying. You wobble, you fall, you get back up. But one day, something clicks, and suddenly you're riding with confidence. Before long, you're no longer thinking about the mechanics—you're simply enjoying the journey, feeling the wind in your hair as you explore new territory.

The invitation stands. *Will you cross over today?*

CHAPTER 6: ⚡🔥 STARTING THE ASCENSION JOURNEY

Proceed with an open heart (and oxygen mask nearby)!

Have you ever watched a toddler discover stairs for the first time? At first, they approach cautiously, uncertain how to navigate this strange new vertical world. Then comes that moment of revelation—they realize they can climb up! Suddenly, their entire perspective changes as they view the world from this new height. Starting your ascension journey is a lot like that—the cautious first steps that lead to an exhilarating new vantage point where everything looks different.

❓ What if the supernatural isn't meant to be extraordinary—but your everyday reality?

After His resurrection, Jesus spent forty days with His disciples, preparing them for the coming of the Holy Spirit and the continuation of His Kingdom work. The Holy Spirit would become their key to unlocking heavenly realms—their invitation to live from their seated position with Christ in heavenly places.

This wasn't an end but a new beginning. Through the Holy Spirit, they received strength, wisdom, and boldness to be His witnesses, equipped with divine power to carry the Gospel with authority. For us too, the Holy

Spirit is our guide into the fullness of union with Christ, empowering us to experience His Kingdom as present reality.

THE DOOR OF ASCENSION

"I am the gate, I am the door; if anyone enters through me, they will be saved." —John 10:9 (NIV)

Jesus reveals Himself not just as the way to salvation, but as a gateway to another realm—a doorway into higher reality. This echoes the beautiful imagery in Song of Solomon: "It was I who took you up the secret stairway of the sky" (Song of Solomon 2:14, TPT). What a picture of ascension—a spiritual journey through Jesus, like Jacob's ladder, where we enter the divine through Him.

Jesus defines salvation itself as entering through Him, the door. This isn't merely a moment of rescue but an invitation into a life of eternal security and spiritual freedom. He promises those who come through Him will "go in and out freely and find green pasture"—a place of endless provision and abundance.

There's profound significance in this promise. Jesus assures us of complete security and offers access to green pastures, symbolizing unlimited sustenance. As the Good Shepherd leads His sheep to pasture, Jesus leads us into a life of provision and safety through the door of salvation and awakening found in Him.

ALIYAH: ASCENDING INTO THE HEAVENLY REALMS

The Hebrew word for ascend, Aliyah, carries a rich meaning: "to go up" or "to ascend." In ancient times, the Israelites made Aliyah when traveling to Jerusalem for sacred feasts, ascending to the city on the hill. In our walk with Christ, Aliyah symbolizes spiritual ascent—our journey into the fullness of God's presence.

This ascent mirrors our spirit's upward journey, transcending earthly limitations to step into divine reality. Through our union with Christ, we participate in His ascension, gaining access to heavenly realms while our physical bodies remain on earth.

What was once a shadow, a yearning to draw near, has become reality in Christ. We are no longer distant or separated; we are one with Him. The veil is torn, the mystery of oneness revealed. Aliyah now means living in the unbroken presence of God, walking in unity with Him, experiencing His Kingdom here and now. No more distance, no more striving—only oneness.

BRINGING HEAVEN TO EARTH

As citizens of Heaven, we're designed for supernatural life. We're called to ascend not only from death to life or doubt to faith, but from earthly limitations into the unlimited possibilities of heavenly realms. As we engage with God's presence and allow His love to transform us, we step into our role as king—priests, carrying His authority, wisdom, and power into the world.

The faith of God connects us to this higher reality, enabling us to live beyond the limitations of time, space, and decay. Heaven isn't a distant place but a present reality, and as we embrace our identity in Christ, we bring the love and power of the Kingdom into every area of our lives. The love of the Kingdom always wins, expanding on earth as Heaven invades our world.

As Justin Paul Abraham teaches, we're called to "agree with Heaven" in our daily lives, aligning our thoughts, words, and actions with the realities of God's Kingdom (*Living in the Realm of the Supernatural*, 2018, p. 42). This agreement creates resonance between Heaven and Earth, allowing divine realities to flow more freely into natural circumstances. When we live from our heavenly identity, miracles, healing, and transformation become the natural outflow of who we are, not just occasional experiences we strive for.

IN HIM: THE KEY TO EVERYTHING

Paul uses the phrase "in Him" (or variations like "in Christ" and "in the Lord") over 160 times throughout his epistles. This phrase is foundational to his theology, emphasizing that everything—from salvation to spiritual growth—flows from our union with Christ.

The phrase "in Him" encapsulates the totality of what it means to belong to Christ:

⁕ It speaks to our union with Christ, through which we share in His death, resurrection, and heavenly position (Ephesians 2:6, NIV)

⁕ It defines our identity as new creations, not by worldly standards but through our relationship with Him (2 Corinthians 5:17, NIV)

⁕ It highlights that all spiritual blessings—redemption, forgiveness, and adoption—are found "in Him" (Ephesians 1:3-7, NIV)

⁕ It is the source of our empowerment, giving us access to divine strength (Philippians 4:13, NIV)

⁕ It points to our transformation, as we are continually molded into the image of Christ (Romans 12:2, NIV)

This profound truth is the key to ascension—to living from heavenly realms while still on earth. Ascension is not a mystical experience reserved for the future but a present reality made possible because we are "in Him." It is in Christ that we live, move, and have our being (Acts 17:28, NKJV, NIV), and through Him we ascend into higher realities of God's Kingdom.

STARTING YOUR ASCENSION JOURNEY

Ascension begins with recognizing our seated position with Christ in heavenly places. This journey of surrender, intimacy, and rest opens us to the realities of God's Kingdom. Through faith, we engage with heavenly realms not as a distant place but as present reality available through our union with Christ.

The Word of God must penetrate beyond our minds into our hearts, transitioning from mere knowledge to true revelation. Whether through sanctified imagination, prayer, or yielding to the Holy Spirit, ascension becomes a practice of encountering God and allowing His presence to transform our lives.

REST AND SURRENDER: THE FOUNDATION OF ASCENSION

Ascension arises from a foundation of Shalom—deep, abiding peace that comes from knowing we are in Christ and He is in us. It begins with profound surrender as we step into the reality that we're already seated with Him in heavenly places. This journey involves no striving or pushing, only simple surrender.

SHALOM: THE GATEWAY TO ASCENSION

Jesus is our peace because peace is a person—He is our shalom, the way into the fullness of life in the Kingdom.

Shalom is far more than the absence of conflict; it represents completeness, wholeness, and well-being in every area of life—spiritual, physical, emotional, and relational. As we walk in shalom, we experience higher Kingdom realities rooted in peace, harmony, and divine order. Living in shalom allows us to ascend, engaging with heavenly realities while demonstrating God's perfect will on earth.

"Throughout the day, I declare shalom over every situation, and it becomes my heart's posture—a constant reminder of the completeness we have in Christ."

This powerful declaration serves as a door into ascension, helping us live in the reality of our lives hidden in Christ, where peace and Kingdom authority flow effortlessly. Through shalom, we live from Heaven to earth, carrying the peace that surpasses understanding (Philippians 4:7, NIV), reflecting God's Kingdom in every aspect of life.

We give Jesus our wholehearted "yes," resting in Him as we open our hearts to receive. We enter the profound truth that we are in Him, and He is in us; we are one. This brings us to the consciousness of our union with Christ—a time to simply be, yield to the Holy Spirit, and experience heavenly realms.

⁜ ASCENSION ACTIVATION: EXPERIENCING UNION WITH CHRIST ⁜

1. Find a quiet place where you won't be disturbed

2. Take several deep breaths, allowing your body and mind to relax

3. Declare: "I am in Christ, and Christ is in me. We are one."

4. Rest in this truth, allowing it to penetrate your heart, not just your mind

5. Ask the Holy Spirit to increase your awareness of your union with Christ

6. Don't strive or push—simply receive the revelation He gives you

7. Journal about your experience afterward

CHILDLIKE FAITH: THE KEY TO ASCENSION

At the beginning of your ascension journey, it's important to give permission to God, offering Him your "yes" and allowing Him to take you wherever He desires. With hearts open to the Holy Spirit, allow Heaven to fill your thoughts and imagination, fully aware that your life is hidden in God.

There are many joyful, childlike ways to enter His presence:

◆ *Divine Embrace:* Imagine giving God a big hug within yourself and feel His embrace in return. This reflects the truth that unless we become like children, we cannot access the Kingdom.

◆ *Humble Posture:* In the Kingdom, the door is in the floor—we must lower ourselves to awaken to His presence. Picture yourself becoming like a small child, safe and secure in the arms of your heavenly Father.

◆ *The Marshmallow of God:* Imagine being completely enveloped in God's presence, surrounded on all sides by His love and protection,

Proceed with a journal in hand (and prepare for divine déjà vu)! Potential side effects include: ✔ Seeing connections where others see coincidences ✔ Experiencing startling moments of clarity in ordinary situations ✔ Spontaneously exclaiming "This is that!" in public places ✔ Developing an addiction to journaling every spiritual impression

like you being a chocolate chip in the marshmallow of God.

◆ *Ocean of Love:* Let yourself fall backward into the ocean of God, sinking into the depths of His love and letting Him fully consume you.

This childlike approach honors the realm of Heaven. What we honor, we attract, and what we focus on, expands. It's a beautiful way to surrender into the realm of love, opening our hearts to encounter the Spirit as we embrace God's presence.

"The truth is that our real lives are hidden in Christ, in God. We are His, this is our eternal placement, so enjoy and engage this profound reality now and receive the infinite resources and nourishment from His table."

ANGELS IN MY JOURNEY OF AWAKENING AND ASCENSION

Throughout my journey of awakening and ascension, angels have played a profound role in bridging my understanding and experience between Heaven and earth. These encounters have deeply shaped my spiritual journey, confirming our true identity and union with Jesus as living gateways for heavenly activity. In humility, I acknowledge that many others have far deeper and more extensive experiences with the angelic realm; what I share here represents only the infancy of this journey for myself and our team.

One particularly powerful experience was during an ascension practice when I had an intense awareness of actually being Jacob's ladder. It felt almost impossible, even bizarre, yet very real—angels were ascending and descending through me, moving freely between heavenly realms from within. Initially, it was challenging to grasp, but as I shared this encounter with the team, we collectively deepened our ascension practice.

This experience resonates deeply with the scriptural reality that, through our union with Jesus, we become living gateways of heavenly realities. In John 1:51, Jesus Himself speaks about angels ascending and descending on the Son of Man. Since we are united with Christ, seated with Him in heavenly places (Ephesians 2:6, NKJV, NIV), and since the

Kingdom is within us (Luke 17:21, NIV), it naturally follows that angels and heavenly beings move freely in and through us.

As I mentioned earlier, during another ascension experience, I clearly saw an "angel of ascension." It was brief yet vivid—I saw the angel fully equipped in mountain climbing gear. Immediately after, I perceived multiple angels around our group, guiding us up Mount Zion. At one point, we experienced something extraordinary: skiing uphill against gravity, symbolizing the supernatural nature of ascending into higher spiritual realms.

Our team frequently experiences angelic presences, not only perceiving their presence but also discerning their names and unique functions in our lives and ministry. These angels are specifically assigned to assist us in fulfilling our divine destinies, guiding, awakening, and empowering us on our spiritual journeys.

Historically, saints and mystics have affirmed this role of angels. St. Thomas Aquinas wrote, "Angels are sent to minister, that is, to assist men in attaining their ultimate end, which is the inheritance of salvation" (*Summa Theologica*, 13th century, I.112.1). Similarly, St. Bernard of Clairvaux emphasized, "Make the holy angels your friends; they are our guides, protectors, and powerful helpers" (*On Consideration*, 12th century, Book V).

CHANTAL'S ANGELIC ENCOUNTER

I live on the East Coast and find prayerful connection on long walks along the ocean shore. During one of these walks, God stopped me with a compelling question: "Who's my government? Where is my government?"

Without hesitation, I replied, "It's me, here I am!" In that moment, God invited me to release His heart's intention over the ocean, calling forth shalom and restoration.

This divine exchange birthed a clear desire and vision in my heart: to acquire a property by the ocean, serving as a physical "legislative office" from which to partner with God in bringing heavenly transformation. Remarkably, within a year, God blessed my family and me with an opportunity to acquire that property. Now, what I affectionately hold in my heart—oneness in God—becomes a tangible place from which to decree transformation and restoration.

During this significant period, I sought the name of the angel actively engaging with me. I distinctly heard, "My name is Mira!" Intrigued, I researched the name's meaning to understand the angel's divine purpose better. To my astonishment and delight, I discovered that Mira means: Admiral, Peace, Female Ruler, and Ocean—each meaning perfectly encapsulating my calling and the divine assignment unfolding in my life.

What we honor, we attract, so we regularly acknowledge the presence of angels even when we cannot perceive them. Together, our experiences with angels reflect a beautiful partnership, unveiling the Kingdom of God on earth and demonstrating the powerful reality of Heaven working through everyday lives surrendered to Christ.

ALINE'S ANGELIC ENCOUNTER

(Aline is Chantal's sister and a member of Flō's spiritual operations team.)

After several days of inviting the Lord to open the eyes of my heart and renew my thoughts (metanoia), I began receiving vivid visions, especially when praying for others. One notable instance occurred when praying for a young woman preparing to share the Word with several groups. I clearly saw an angel standing beside her. While I had previously seen spiritual realities, angels were new territory. When I asked the Lord about this angel, He revealed that the angel always stood by her when addressing crowds, imparting boldness and strength. This angel kept his hand on her shoulder, steadfast in his assignment.

His name was Conrad, and his role was specifically to prepare hearts to receive.

In another encounter, as I prayed for a businessman, the Lord showed me an impressive angel made entirely of silver metal, with wings composed of multiple swords. God explained that this angel was designated to execute His justice and law over territories we entrusted to Him. Later, this angel's existence and function were independently confirmed by others who had also seen him.

At my workplace, Flō's office, I encountered an angel energetically swirling around me. The Lord explained that this was Flō's angel, the angel of plants and greenery, tasked with overseeing everything green, nurturing budding life and vegetation that provides essential nutrients.

One of the most awe-inspiring experiences occurred while praying for our nation and a specific city. When I asked the Lord about the angelic presence over the city, I was transported spiritually and stood alongside a magnificent angel, appearing like a hybrid of man and bird. His majestic appearance resembled dark wheat, detailed in heavenly attire. His wings remained open, releasing a resonance like an ultrasound, echoing the heartbeat of an unborn child. Each wingbeat scattered grains of wheat onto the ground, symbolizing sowing hope and new life. This profound encounter filled me with overwhelming hope and wonder, demonstrating once more the incredible partnership God invites us into with His angelic hosts.

Together, these experiences reveal our beautiful partnership with Heaven, affirming our roles as gateways for God's Kingdom to manifest powerfully in our everyday lives.

☺ Reflection Questions:

❓ How does recognizing your role as a living gateway reshape your spiritual expectations?

? How can you practically engage more intentionally with angels in your daily ascension practices?

UNION WITH CHRIST: THE NEW JACOB'S LADDER

With the Holy Spirit, engaging the spirit realm becomes a holy and beautiful experience. Jesus said: "I am the Way, the Truth, and the Life. No one comes next to the Father except through union with Me" (John 14:6, TPT).

This union grants us access to heavenly realms, making us the new Jacob's ladder, connecting Heaven and earth (John 1:51, NIV). This is entirely Christ's accomplishment, not ours! In Jacob's vision (Genesis 28:12, NIV), the ladder represented a connection between earthly and heavenly realms, with angels ascending and descending. Through Christ, this connection is now made in and through us, enabling heavenly realities to touch earth. We are now the temple of God, the meeting point between Heaven and earth. We are the house of God!

Every believer is a "burning one"—a living temple where Heaven and earth converge. Our bodies are the dwelling place of God, where His glory is manifested. As we embrace our identity as temples of the Holy Spirit, we become living gateways for the Kingdom to flow through, bringing Heaven's realities into every situation.

DAILY SURRENDER: THE GATEWAY TO ASCENSION

My journey into intimacy with God began with simple steps—seeking Him, engaging with His Word, spending time in prayer, and connecting with believers. As I made time for God, my awareness of His presence grew, and hunger for Him deepened. Transitioning from an orphan mindset to embracing my identity as a son transformed what once felt like effort into an effortless, joyful pursuit, free from religious obligations.

Over time, seeking Him evolved into a lifestyle of honoring Him. This shifted me from self-focus to God-focus, naturally leading to greater concern for others. A key element has been daily yielding to God, surrendering every part of myself afresh to Him each day.

When I begin my day, I consciously surrender to God, inviting Him into my thoughts, imagination, and life. I declare, "Not my will, but Your will be done," and pray for a fresh baptism of His Spirit. I ask for His holy, refining fire to burn away anything hindering my relationship with Him and set my heart ablaze with passion. This daily surrender opens me to deeper sensitivity to the Holy Spirit, guiding my thoughts, actions, and prayers.

♦ **Practical Daily Surrender:**

1. Begin each day by consciously yielding to God

2. Invite the Holy Spirit to guide your thoughts, decisions, and actions

3. Declare your dependence on God rather than your own strength

4. Release control of your day's outcomes to Him

5. Ask for a fresh awareness of His presence throughout the day and declare in me He lives and moves and has His being

THE FEAR OF THE LORD AND INTIMACY WITH GOD

As I continue yielding to God and experiencing Him more deeply, the spirit of the fear of the Lord grows stronger in my life. This profound reverence brings greater awe and wonder of who He is. Part of fearing the Lord is beginning to love what God loves and hate what God hates. Things I once enjoyed now seem unimaginable to me. It's a transformative experience shaping how I live, causing me to walk in humility and thanksgiving.

I've found that one of the greatest ways to cultivate intimacy with God is through thanksgiving. I make a conscious effort to give thanks at every meal and throughout my day—mindful of little things and everything He's doing in my life. Everything is by the grace of God, and gratitude is key to staying aligned with His heart.

ENGAGING GOD'S PRESENCE IN EVERYDAY MOMENTS

This intimacy means constant awareness of God's presence. From the moment I open my eyes, I talk to Him throughout the day, knowing He is with me in everything. Whether in joy or suffering, I lean on Him as my strength, comfort, and joy. I've invited Him into my heart, my hurts and pains, and experienced profound healing encounters with Jesus.

I used to be emotionally unavailable and guarded, making intimacy with God difficult, but inner healing has been a game-changer, allowing me to open my heart fully to Him.

As I yield to the Holy Spirit daily, I continuously go deeper into the Spirit's realms. This intimacy transforms mundane into sacred—whether feeding birds, enjoying morning coffee, or working at my desk, I sense His presence and love in every moment. His love flows through me to others. I often find myself becoming an answer to someone's prayer, led by the Spirit to bring hope and encouragement.

A LIFESTYLE OF WORSHIP AND CONTINUOUS COMMUNION

Living in intimacy with God isn't just a practice; it's an ongoing adventure. It's a lifestyle of worship—a heart seeking to glorify God. By surrendering daily and inviting Him into every part of my life, I experience His guidance, love, and presence in profound ways. This journey involves continually engaging with His Spirit, going deeper into His heart, and living in the fullness of His Kingdom here and now. Living in intimacy with God means recognizing He is my "All in all," making every aspect of life an act of worship.

? **Wonder Question:**

? How can you cultivate the same deep intimacy with God that New Testament figures experienced, allowing you to access heavenly realms in your own spiritual journey?

As you begin your own ascension journey, remember that learning to enter heavenly realms is like learning to swim—at first, you might splash around awkwardly, but with practice, you'll soon be gliding effortlessly through depths you once feared. The key is to start where you are, with simple childlike faith, knowing that God is eager to meet you in every sincere attempt to connect with Him.

Will you take your first steps up Heaven's stairway today?

BONUS: THE BREATH OF HEAVEN—A GATEWAY TO ASCENSION

⚠️ WARNING: This Chapter May Revolutionize Your Next Breath 🚨

Proceed with both feet on the ground (though your spirit may soar higher with each inhale)!

Potential side effects include: ✅ Finding spiritual significance in an activity you've taken for granted ✅ Experiencing Heaven's reality through a simple inhale and exhale ✅ Never breathing the same way again

❓ What if the simplest act you perform thousands of times daily is actually your most powerful tool for spiritual ascension?

THE DIVINE RHYTHM: BREATHING AS SPIRITUAL PRACTICE

Breathing is our most fundamental act—yet hidden within this automatic function lies a profound spiritual gateway. With each inhale and exhale, we're participating in the rhythm of creation itself, echoing the very breath God used to animate humanity in Genesis 2:7 when He "breathed into his nostrils the breath of life."

THE MIRACLE OF DIVINE DESIGN

Consider the wonder of what happens with every breath you take:

Your lungs—if spread out fully—would cover a tennis court in surface area, a masterpiece of divine engineering hidden within your chest. Each breath delivers life-giving oxygen to approximately 40 trillion cells through an intricate network of blood vessels stretching nearly 60,000 miles—enough to circle the earth twice with room to spare!

? **Wonder Question:**

? When was the last time you paused to marvel at the miracle that your body processes roughly 11,000 liters of air every day without you giving it a single conscious thought?

This isn't merely biological efficiency—it's sacred architecture. The same God who crafted the cosmos with mathematical precision designed your respiratory system as a living testimony to His attention to detail and care. Your breathing is both ordinary and extraordinary—a mundane function and a magnificent miracle.

When we breathe mindfully, our bodies activate the parasympathetic nervous system—God's built-in restoration mechanism that calms our nervous system, reduces stress hormones, and creates inner stillness. Physiologically, deep breathing transforms us from a state of anxiety to a state of peace—from fight-or-flight to rest-and-receive.

This physical shift creates the perfect conditions for spiritual ascension.

? **Wonder Question:**

? What if the veil between Heaven and earth is as thin as the membrane in your lungs that exchanges oxygen and carbon dioxide—just one cell thick?

BREATHING THE NAME OF GOD

Consider this revelation that has transformed believers for centuries: the sacred name of God—YHWH (Yahweh)—is actually composed of breath sounds:

- "Yah" (inhale)
- "Weh" (exhale)

Every time you breathe, you're literally speaking the holy name of God! Your most automatic function is a continuous, involuntary acknowledgment of your Creator. As Psalm 150:6 declares, "Let everything that has breath praise the Lord!" Your very breathing is praise—a constant communion with the Divine.

? **Wonder Question:**

? If you breathe approximately 23,000 times per day, how might your life change if you became conscious that you're speaking God's name with each breath?

This understanding transforms breathing from a mere biological function into a sacred gateway of connection with God.

TRINITARIAN BREATHING: INHALING HEAVEN'S ATMOSPHERE

⫶ The Practice of Trinitarian Breathing ⫶

When you intentionally breathe, you're not just taking in oxygen—you're inhaling the very atmosphere of Heaven. This practice helps shift your consciousness from earthly awareness to heavenly perspective:

1. Find a quiet space where you can be still for 5-10 minutes

2. Close your eyes and take three deep, cleansing breaths

3. As you inhale, visualize yourself drawing in the triune nature of God:

   - The Father's perfect love
   - The Son's transforming grace
   - The Spirit's empowering presence

4. As you exhale, release:

   - Fear and anxiety
   - Performance and striving
   - Earthly limitations

5. With each breath, silently declare:

   - Inhale: "I receive Your heavenly life"
   - Exhale: "I release earthly thinking"

6. Continue this rhythm until you sense a shift in your awareness—a lightness, peace, or heightened sensitivity to God's presence

This practice prepares your whole being—spirit, soul, and body—for ascension experiences by aligning your consciousness with heavenly realities.

? **Wonder Question:**

? What would happen if your consciousness became as expansive as the oxygen molecules that flow through every cell of your body, touching places you didn't even know existed within you?

BREATHING AS CONSCIOUSNESS SHIFT

Chantal describes her experience with this practice:

"When I practice Trinitarian breathing, I find myself naturally ascending into greater awareness of God's presence. It's as if each breath thins the veil between Heaven and earth, allowing me to perceive both realms simultaneously. What begins as a simple breathing exercise often becomes a profound encounter with God's throne room reality."

This aligns with what the early church father Maximus the Confessor taught: "The soul ascends not by physical movement but by the awakening of spiritual consciousness" (*Centuries on Love*, 2:26, 7th century). Breathing mindfully creates the conditions for this awakening to occur naturally, without striving.

? **Wonder Question:**

? If your breath can exchange carbon dioxide for oxygen at the cellular level, what divine exchanges might be happening in your spirit with each conscious breath you take?

THE SCIENCE OF SACRED BREATHING

Modern science confirms what spiritual practitioners have known for millennia: controlled breathing directly affects brain function. When we breathe deeply and rhythmically:

◆ Alpha brain waves increase, associated with heightened awareness and creativity ◆ The prefrontal cortex calms, reducing analytical thinking and opening intuitive perception ◆ The limbic system relaxes, allowing emotional barriers to spiritual experience to dissolve

These physiological changes create the perfect conditions for spiritual perception—allowing your spirit to move beyond bodily limitations and engage with heavenly realities.

PRACTICAL APPLICATION: THE 5-5-5 BREATH OF HEAVEN

This simple but powerful practice can be done anywhere, anytime:

1. Breathe in for five seconds——Inhaling Father's love, Son's grace, Spirit's power

2. Hold for five seconds——Allowing Heaven's atmosphere to fill every part of your being

3. Breathe out for five seconds——Releasing earthly concerns, anxieties, and limitations

Practice this rhythm for just 3-5 minutes, and you'll be amazed at how quickly your spiritual awareness heightens and your consciousness shifts toward heavenly realities.

? Wonder Question:

? How might your relationship with God transform if you approached each breath as a holy exchange—a sacred conversation between Creator and created?

BREATH DECLARATIONS: SPEAKING HEAVEN INTO EARTH

The simple act of breathing can become a powerful portal into heavenly realms when paired with declarations of truth. As you practice sacred breathing, allow these declarations to amplify your awareness of the divine reality that surrounds you and dwells within you:

⚜ Union Declarations

- "In Him I live and move and have my being" (Acts 17:28, NKJV)
- "Christ in me, the hope of glory" (Colossians 1:27)
- "I am in Christ, and Christ is in me—we are one"
- "As Jesus is, so am I in this world" (1 John 4:17)

Position Declarations

- "With each breath, I am more aware of my seated position in Christ"
- "I am already seated with Christ in heavenly places" (Ephesians 2:6, NKJV)
- "I breathe in heavenly perspective and exhale earthly limitations"
- "My consciousness is being lifted into alignment with Heaven's reality"

Gateway Declarations

- "I am a living gateway where Heaven's atmosphere flows into Earth"
- "My life is the meeting place of Heaven and Earth"
- "Through me, the Kingdom comes and God's will is done"
- "I release the fragrance of Christ with every exhale"

Reality Declarations

- "The veil is torn—I see clearly now what has always been true"
- "I shift from earth-consciousness to Heaven-consciousness"
- "I am awakening to the truth that Heaven is my native realm"
- "The Kingdom of God is within me, expanding into all I touch" (Luke 17:21)

As you breathe deeply, allow these truths to penetrate beyond mental understanding into the very fabric of your being. With each inhale, receive Heaven's life; with each exhale, release Heaven's reality into the atmosphere around you.

Remember what Chantal discovered—you don't have to do anything to ascend; you simply need to give God permission. These breath declarations create space for that divine awareness to expand within you, aligning your consciousness with the truth of your heavenly citizenship.

Practice this for just a few minutes each day, and watch how your awareness of heavenly realities grows, transforming not just your perception but your very experience of life itself.

THE BREATH THAT CONNECTS ALL CREATION

Your breathing connects you not only to God but to all creation. The oxygen molecules you inhale today may have been exhaled by ancient redwoods, cycled through ocean currents, or carried on winds across continents. This interconnectedness mirrors the spiritual reality that we are all one in Christ, breathing the same divine breath that animates all life.

? **Wonder Question:**

? If you share breath molecules with every person who has ever lived, how might that transform how you see your connection to the global body of Christ across time and space?

REFLECTION AND ACTIVATION

✷ **Reflection Question:**

? How might incorporating intentional sacred breathing transform your daily spiritual life and ascension experiences?

Breathing Activation: Right now, take one minute to practice Trinitarian breathing. Focus completely on inhaling Heaven's atmosphere and exhaling earthly thinking. Notice any shifts in your awareness, peace levels, or spiritual sensitivity.

Wonder Practice: The next time you take a deep breath, pause to wonder at the miracle happening within you. Let that wonder lead you into worship of the God who designed both your physical breathing and your spiritual capacity for communion with Him.

Remember, ascension isn't complicated—it begins with the simplest act of awakening to (sensitize) Heaven's reality Heaven's reality into your consciousness. This practice doesn't just prepare you for ascension; it is ascension itself—a continuous awakening to the reality that Heaven's atmosphere is already within and around you.

As Richard Rohr reminds us, "The spiritual life is not about getting somewhere else; it's about becoming aware of where we already are" (*Everything Belongs,* 2003, p. 28).

Start with breath. Awaken to Heaven. Transform the Earth.

FROM PRACTICE TO NATURAL LIVING

Just as a child learning to walk eventually runs without thinking about each step, your journey into the ascended life will gradually become as natural as breathing. What begins as intentional practice will transform into your default way of being. There will come a point where you no longer need techniques, steps, or even conscious effort to live from your heavenly position.

As Justin Paul Abraham teaches, "The ascended life isn't about achieving a spiritual state—it's about awakening to what has always been true of you" (*Beyond Human,* 2017, p. 42). When this awakening fully penetrates your consciousness, you'll find yourself naturally thinking Heaven's thoughts, speaking Heaven's language, and manifesting Heaven's reality without striving.

The declarations and breathing practices are like training wheels—helpful for a season but eventually unnecessary as you learn to ride freely in your true identity. In time, your awareness of heavenly realities will be so integrated that you'll move seamlessly between realms, carrying Heaven's atmosphere as effortlessly as you carry your own presence.

Practice this for just a few minutes each day, and watch how your awareness of heavenly realities grows, transforming not just your perception but your very experience of life itself.

CHAPTER 7: ✨🔥 ENCOUNTERING THE HEAVENLY REALMS

☀️ WARNING: This Chapter May Cause Unexpected
Dimension Shifts ☀️

Proceed with both feet on the ground (though your spirit may not stay there)!

Potential side effects include: ✅ Seeing angelic activity during your morning commute ✅ Accidentally responding to invisible realities in public places ✅ Being suspiciously peaceful in chaos-inducing situations ✅ Finding yourself more fascinated with unseen things than Netflix

Imagine walking through airport security and suddenly realizing you've been carrying an entire ocean in your water bottle. That's what discovering Heaven's accessibility feels like—you've been carrying infinite reality within you all along, and somehow nobody noticed! The surprising truth is that the extraordinary realm we've been seeking isn't hidden behind complex spiritual techniques or reserved for the super-spiritual—it's been hiding in plain sight, waiting for us to simply open our eyes.

? What if the veil between Heaven and earth is thinner than you've ever imagined?

Throughout history, believers have experienced profound encounters with heavenly realms while still living on earth.

BIBLICAL FOUNDATIONS OF ASCENSION

The Bible is filled with examples of people who experienced heavenly realities while still on earth:

⁘ Jesus' Ascension opened the way for the Holy Spirit to empower all believers to engage with heavenly realities (Acts 1:9-11, NIV)

⁘ Stephen, facing martyrdom, gazed into Heaven and saw Christ standing at God's right hand—showing how Heaven's realm becomes accessible when we yield to the Spirit (Acts 7:55-56, NIV)

⁘ Paul's journey to "the third heaven" reveals that profound heavenly experiences are part of our spiritual inheritance (2 Corinthians 12:2-4, NIV)

⁘ John heard "come up here" and was instantly transported to the throne room—demonstrating how the Spirit enables us to transcend natural limitations (Revelation 4:1-2, NIV)

⁘ Peter's vision led to the inclusion of Gentiles in the church—revealing how heavenly encounters guide God's purposes on earth (Acts 10, NIV)

These biblical examples show that experiencing heavenly realms isn't extraordinary—it's the normal Christian life Jesus intended for all believers.

THE KINGDOM WITHIN AND ABOVE: TWO SIDES OF ONE REALITY

"For God's kingdom realm is already expanding within some of you."
—Luke 17:21 (TPT)

This profound truth reveals the dual nature of ascension—it is both an inward reality and an upward journey. When we speak of "going up," we're ascending into a higher reality that already exists within us through our union with Christ.

Think of it like a radio—the music is always broadcasting, but you need to tune your receiver to the right frequency. Similarly, Heaven's realities are always present, but we need to align our spiritual senses to perceive them.

This heavenly realm is the source from which all things are created and sustained (Colossians 1:16-17, NIV). By living from this higher reality, we align ourselves with the eternal truths of the Kingdom, bringing Heaven's realities into our earthly experience.

? **Wonder Questions:**

? What might change in your daily life if you began to perceive the heavenly realm that's already surrounding you?

? How would your prayers, relationships, and work be transformed?

PROPHETIC VISION AND REVELATION

Engaging with heavenly realms involves shifting our awareness to the Spirit and living in constant awareness of our union with Jesus. This flows from surrender and intimacy with God.

Just as Joel prophesied: "I will pour out my Spirit on everybody and cause your sons and daughters to prophesy, and your young men will see visions, and your old men will experience dreams from God" (Acts 2:17, TPT).

This highlights that supernatural visions, dreams, and prophecy are normal experiences for all believers in these last days—not just for a select few. He is falling on all flesh! The question is not whether these experiences are available, but whether we're positioned to receive them.

MODERN GUIDES FOR THE JOURNEY

Many contemporary teachers are helping believers reclaim their inheritance of heavenly experiences. Three who have particularly influenced our journey at Flō are:

Liz Wright – Following a physical visitation from Jesus in 1995, Liz has helped countless people understand their seated position with Christ. She teaches that the ascended life means being continually aware of where we're already positioned in Christ, which empowers us to manifest God's Kingdom on earth (Living From a Place of Rest, 2018, p. 42).

Liz often says: "Heaven isn't waiting for us—we're seated there now. Our journey is about becoming aware of where we already are."

Justin Paul Abraham – Justin's teachings have opened our eyes to joy and supernatural living as our inheritance in Christ. He often calls Earth "planet joy," encouraging believers to agree with God's plans here and now (*Beyond Human*, 2017, p. 89).

For Justin, ascension involves tangibly engaging with heavenly realms—stepping into the joy of divine encounters and bringing that reality into everyday life. He describes shifting consciousness (renewing our minds) to the spiritual realm to receive solutions for earthly situations.

Nancy Cohen – Nancy emphasizes accessing heavenly courts and partnering with God in divine governance. For her, believers are meant to engage with Heaven's resources and bring them to earth-fulfilling our role as co-laborers with Christ (*Engaging Heaven's Court*, 2020, p. 37).

She teaches that every believer can "ascend and descend in the Spirit," seeing "things that were, things that are, and things yet to come" as they participate in God's restoration of all things.

All three teachers agree that ascension involves both spiritual encounters and living from heavenly authority—bringing Heaven's realities to earth.

LIVING IN CONTINUOUS COMMUNION

In Chantal's own words:

Heavenly encounters aren't limited to dramatic moments—they can happen in the midst of everyday life. In my experience, God's presence in ordinary tasks—vacuuming, shopping, brushing my hair—becomes an ongoing conversation with Him.

This practice of continual awareness makes divine communion possible in the most ordinary activities. I've found that hearing God's guidance during simple moments happens naturally when we live in continuous awareness of His presence.

"From the moment I open my eyes, I talk with Him and engage with Him throughout the day, knowing He is with me in everything. Whether in joy or suffering, I lean on Him as my strength, comfort, and joy."

THE SURPRISING PATHWAY THROUGH SUFFERING

Counterintuitively, suffering often becomes a doorway to deeper spiritual experience. I've experienced God most profoundly during seasons of financial struggles, health issues, and feelings of abandonment.

Similarly, in Bryan's journey through the devastating loss of his daughter and a three-year murder trial, he discovered that suffering can become a surprising portal into heavenly realities.

"So I'm not defeated by my weakness, but delighted! For my weakness becomes a portal to God's power." —2 Corinthians 12:10 (TPT)

The paradoxical truth is that our weakest moments can become our most powerful opportunities to experience divine reality. When all human strength fails, our spirits often become more receptive to Heaven's presence.

THE YIELDING PROCESS: FOUNDATION FOR KINGDOM LIVING

Everything in the Kingdom begins with yielding—surrendering to Jesus as Lord establishes the foundation for transformed living. The lifestyle of yielding embraces continuous repentance (metanoia)—not just turning from sin but constantly turning toward God.

This complete shift in perspective helps us think as Heaven thinks. It's like learning a new language—at first, it's awkward and difficult, but eventually you begin to think in the new language naturally.

BAPTISM OF FIRE: A LIFE SET ABLAZE

John the Baptist prophesied that Jesus would baptize with "the Holy Spirit and fire" (Matthew 3:11, NIV). This baptism is both spiritually transformative and often experienced in tangible ways.

This fire serves two purposes:

1. It burns away impurities that hinder our relationship with God

2. It ignites deeper passion for Him, setting our hearts ablaze

Fire falls on sacrifice, and as we submit our lives as living sacrifices (Romans 12:1, NIV), we invite God's transformative fire. The more we yield to this fire, the more we become carriers of His presence.

PRACTICAL STEPS TO BEGIN YOUR ASCENSION JOURNEY

1. *Set Aside Sacred Space and Time*: Create a daily appointment to be still and aware of God's presence. Even ten or fifteen minutes can become a gateway to heavenly encounters.

2. *Declare Your Position in Christ*: Regularly affirm: "I am seated with Christ in heavenly places" (Ephesians 2:6, NKJV, NIV). This isn't creating something new but acknowledging what's already true.

3. *Engage Your Sanctified Imagination*: Your imagination is a God-given tool for perceiving spiritual realities. Ask the Holy Spirit to guide your visualization of heavenly truths.

4. *Journal Your Experiences*: Record even small impressions or encounters. Over time, you'll recognize patterns in how God communicates with you.

5. *Find Community*: Share your journey with others who are also exploring heavenly realities. Their faith will strengthen yours, and your testimonies will encourage them.

6. *Study Scripture with Fresh Eyes*: Read familiar passages asking, "What heavenly reality is this revealing?" Let the Word become a doorway to encounter, not just information.

7. *Embrace Childlike Faith*: Jesus said the Kingdom belongs to those who receive it like children (Matthew 18:3, NIV). Wonder, trust, and simplicity open doors that sophistication cannot.

8. *Practice Declaring Shalom*: Declare God's peace over situations and people, recognizing that this peace is more than the absence of conflict—it's the presence of wholeness.

9. *Recognize God in Ordinary Moments*: Train yourself to see divine presence in everyday life—a sunset, a conversation, a moment of insight.

10. *Yield Daily to the Holy Spirit*: Begin each day with surrender: "Not my will, but Yours be done." This posture of yielding creates space for Heaven to manifest through your life.

ASCENSION ACTIVATION: DAILY PRESENCE PRACTICE

1. Set aside five or ten minutes at the beginning of your day

2. Find a quiet place where you won't be disturbed

3. Begin by acknowledging your position: "Lord, I am seated with You in heavenly places"

4. Take several deep breaths, releasing anxiety and welcoming peace

5. Ask the Holy Spirit to heighten your awareness of heavenly realities around you

6. As you go through your day, set reminders (perhaps when you check your phone or drink water) to pause and reconnect with Heaven's reality

7. At day's end, journal any moments where you sensed Heaven's presence or received divine insight

THE FIRE OF GOD'S PURPOSE

The path of yielding, trusting, and leaning into God rather than performing or striving is about finding God's will not in extraordinary events but in the simple act of surrender to divine love, moment by moment.

As Chantal beautifully expresses: "The most beautiful things that have happened in my life were through yielding and surrendering to His living flame of Love!" The central insight of spiritual life through the ages is that union with God comes not through achievement but through surrender.

YOUR INVITATION TO ASCEND

The journey of ascension isn't about reaching some distant spiritual pinnacle but about awakening to where you already are in Christ.

Will you say yes to discovering the limitless realities of God's Kingdom? Will you yield to His Spirit and allow Him to guide you into deeper dimensions of His presence? Will you embrace childlike faith and wonder as you explore the vastness of His love?

Remember, ascension isn't about striving—it's about surrendering. It's not about earning—it's about receiving. It's not about getting somewhere new—it's about awakening to where you already are.

Think of it like a person who has lived their entire life in a house with the curtains drawn, never realizing they have an ocean view just outside their window. The ocean was always there—they just needed to pull back the curtains to see it. Your heavenly perspective isn't something you need to achieve; it's a reality you simply need to recognize.

The doorway is open. The Spirit is calling. Heaven is waiting.

Will you step in?

CHAPTER 8: ✨🔥HEROES OF FAITH—LIVING AS CITIZENS OF HEAVEN NOW

🚨 WARNING: This Chapter May Cause Heroic
Side Effects 🚨

Proceed with cape ready (supernatural powers may activate at any moment)!

Potential side effects include: ✅ Suddenly viewing "impossible" situations as divine opportunities ✅ Developing an unhealthy disregard for natural limitations ✅ Spontaneously pulling heavenly realities into everyday circumstances ✅ Finding yourself mentioned in future faith hall-of-fame lists

Have you ever watched a child dressed as a superhero? They don't pretend to have powers—in their minds, they truly believe they can fly, shoot webs, or lift cars. Their faith in their identity is absolute and unwavering. The heroes of our faith weren't so different—they simply refused to see limitations where others saw impossibilities. They didn't just read about heavenly citizenship; they lived as though their heavenly passport was the only identification that mattered.

? What if the most powerful examples of heavenly living aren't found in the future, but in our spiritual history?

Throughout Scripture and church history, we find men and women who lived as though seated in heavenly places—not as a theological concept, but as their daily reality. These heroes of faith demonstrate what's possible when we bring Heaven's authority, resources, and power into every situation.

FAITH THAT PULLS HEAVEN INTO EARTH

"Through faith's power they conquered kingdoms and established true justice. Their faith fastened onto their promises and pulled them into reality!" —Hebrews 11:32-33 (TPT)

Faith has always been the foundation upon which God's people stand. The heroes showcased in Scripture weren't just historical figures but living testimonies of what it means to trust God amid impossible circumstances. They demonstrated a profound truth: God's power manifests through those who believe.

Their stories teach us that the same God who parted seas, raised the dead, and brought nations to victory still works through His people's faith today. Their examples provide a blueprint for how we can walk in the power of God's promises and manifest Heaven's realities now.

THREE EXTRAORDINARY EXAMPLES

Let's examine three key heroes who exemplified extraordinary faith, living as though God's future promises were already manifested in their present.

196

1. *Enoch: The First Ascension*

"By faith Enoch was taken from this life, so that he did not experience death: 'He could not be found, because God had taken him away.' For before he was taken, he was commended as one who pleased God."
—Hebrews 11:5 (NIV)

Living 3,000 years before Christ, Enoch demonstrated an extraordinary walk with God. In a time of widespread wickedness, his communion with God was so profound that he bypassed death entirely, being translated directly into Heaven (Genesis 5:24, NIV).

Scripture tells us he "walked with God" for 300 years before his translation. This wasn't merely metaphorical but represented intimate communion and alignment with God's heart. Enoch's life was so synchronized with Heaven's reality that the boundary between worlds dissolved.

I was listening to a podcast where Justin Paul Abraham beautifully described walking with God as "hand in hand, in and out, to and fro" (*Beyond Human*, 2018, p. 124).

Enoch shows us the limitless possibilities available to those who walk intimately with God. If he could access such divine realities before Christ's redemptive work, how much more should we, as believers united with Christ, live in the Kingdom's fullness now?

His story challenges our limited expectations of what's possible. His very existence confronts the idea that supernatural experience is rare—rather, it demonstrates that profound spiritual experiences naturally flow from walking closely with God.

? Wonder Question:

? What might happen if you began to walk in such intimate communion with God that, like Enoch, Heaven's realities became more real to you than earthly limitations?

2. *David: Prophetic Insight into Future Grace*

David, a man after God's own heart, accessed Messianic promises over 1,000 years before Christ's coming. His prophetic Psalms, particularly Psalm 22 and Psalm 110, not only foreshadowed Christ's crucifixion and eternal reign but demonstrated how David's faith allowed him to perceive future realities and pull them into his present.

"I see that the LORD is always with me. I will not be shaken, for he is right beside me... For you will not leave my soul among the dead or allow your Holy One to rot in the grave." —Psalm 16:8-10 (NLT)

David's plea in Psalm 51 for a clean heart wasn't merely personal prayer but prophetic anticipation of the grace and renewal that would come through Jesus. His life testifies to how faith opens doorways for God's future promises to manifest in the present.

Potential side effects include: ✅ Finding yourself thinking in heavenly dimensions while grocery shopping ✅ Accidentally speaking angelic languages during business meetings ✅ Developing an unshakable peace that confuses your anxious friends ✅ Spotting divine doorways in ordinary places

David experienced divine ascension not as disengagement from the world but deeper engagement with reality as God sees it. Amid battles, political struggles, and personal failures, his ability to access Heaven's perspective enabled him to navigate earthly challenges from a heavenly vantage point.

David's psalms are portals into divine encounters, inviting us to experience what he experienced—the joy, the fire, the presence, and the revelation of God. His ability to step into future redemptive realities through worship and prophetic revelation demonstrates how ascension enables us to collapse time and access Kingdom truths that exist outside our linear experience.

3. *Elisha: Demonstrating Kingdom Realities*

Elisha lived a life characterized by miraculous demonstrations of God's power that pointed forward to the Messiah's coming. His ministry included multiplying food, raising the dead, and healing the sick—not as isolated events but as glimpses of God's future Kingdom made present.

When Elisha asked for a double portion of Elijah's spirit, he sought increased capacity to demonstrate God's Kingdom on earth. This request wasn't merely about power but expanding his ability to bring Heaven to earth tangibly. The dramatic miracles that followed—from parting rivers to raising the dead—showed what happens when one person fully yields to God's Spirit.

Even more remarkably, Elisha's very bones carried such Kingdom authority that a dead man thrown into his tomb was resurrected upon touching them (2 Kings 13:21, NIV). This extraordinary event reveals how deeply God's life-giving power had permeated Elisha's being—to the point that even his physical remains carried resurrection power.

When we align with Heaven's perspective and authority, like Elisha, we become conduits of supernatural power. The greater works Jesus promised are meant to be our normal experience as we learn to operate from our seated position with Christ.

FAITH DEMONSTRATED IN THE FIRE

One of the most powerful Old Testament examples of faith in action is the story of Shadrach, Meshach, and Abednego. These three men faced an impossible choice—bow to Nebuchadnezzar's golden statue or face a fiery furnace. They refused to compromise, boldly declaring their God could deliver them. But even if He didn't, they would remain faithful.

"If we are thrown into the blazing furnace, the God we serve is able to deliver us from it, and he will deliver us from Your Majesty's hand. But even if he does not, we want you to know, Your Majesty, that we will not serve your gods or worship the image of gold you have set up." —Daniel 3:17-18 (NIV)

The furnace was heated seven times hotter than usual—so intense it killed the soldiers who threw them in. Yet these three men walked unharmed amid the flames, joined by a fourth figure like "the Son of God." When Nebuchadnezzar called them out, they emerged without a burn, their clothes untouched, not even smelling of smoke (Daniel 3:27, NIV).

This story illustrates a profound truth: what we focus on expands. These men focused not on the fire's intensity but on God's faithfulness. Their faith rested not in their ability to avoid flames but in God's power to sustain them through the flames.

The story presents a powerful picture of ascension in the midst of fiery trials. When we stand firm in our heavenly identity, refusing to bow to earthly pressure, we create space for Heaven to invade earth in miraculous ways. The fourth man's appearance demonstrates how our faithfulness in trials creates an environment where Christ's presence manifests tangibly.

OUR GREATER INHERITANCE

Jesus made an extraordinary statement in Matthew 11:11: "For I tell you the truth, throughout history there has never been a man who surpasses John the Baptizer. Yet the least of those who now experience heaven's kingdom realm will become even greater than he" (TPT).

This reveals the incredible privilege we have as part of Heaven's Kingdom. Through our union with Christ, we have access to a level of spiritual authority and intimacy with God surpassing even the greatest Old Testament heroes' experiences.

The saints of old saw the glory of God as if looking at a veiled light, but we who have received the Holy Spirit see the glory of God unveiled. Jesus went to the Father and sent the Spirit to continue His mission and empower us to do even greater miracles than He displayed on earth!

Our spiritual inheritance as sons and daughters is mind-boggling! Through our union with Christ, we're empowered with the same explosive power that enabled the Old Testament heroes to accomplish great things for God. The significant difference is that while God's Spirit came upon them at specific times, we are now God's house, with His Spirit dwelling within us permanently.

"Now, my beloved ones, I have saved these most important truths for last: Be supernaturally infused with strength through your life-union with the Lord Jesus. Stand victorious with the force of His explosive power flowing in and through you!" —Ephesians 6:10 (TPT)

We're not just receivers of power—we are carriers of God's very presence. The same power that raised Christ from the dead dwells in us, making us walking portals of Heaven's reality.

PULLING THE FUTURE INTO THE NOW

Faith is the substance connecting us to the unseen—the bridge that pulls Heaven's promises into the now. As Hebrews 11:1 (TPT) declares, "Now faith brings our hopes into reality and becomes the foundation needed to acquire the things we long for. It is all the evidence required to prove what is still unseen."

The heroes of faith in Hebrews 11:33 "fastened onto their promises and pulled them into reality." They reached into the future and brought Heaven's promises into their present, transforming their reality with Heaven's power. What's remarkable is that many died without seeing the complete fulfillment of what they believed for—this makes their steadfast trust even more inspiring.

Faith itself comes from God. As we grow in our understanding of His love for us, faith naturally increases. It flows not from our striving but from resting in His perfect love and our redeemed innocence in Him.

This faith empowers us to move beyond what our natural eyes perceive, drawing on the invisible realities of God's Kingdom. Remember, God's Kingdom isn't just a distant, future hope—it's a present experience. As Heaven's citizens, we're invited to experience the fullness of God's presence, power, and love in tangible, life-changing ways right now.

FAITH AS A SUPERNATURAL FORCE

Chantal beautifully describes faith as a superpower God has placed within us:

"Faith is like a superpower God placed within you. When you put your faith in Jesus, it activates and brings into existence what doesn't yet exist! Faith is like a vehicle, transporting from Heaven's realm into the physical realm. Faith actualizes what it realizes! Faith creates and births on earth things no eyes have seen nor ears heard, as our gaze focuses on the Author of our faith."

She shares a powerful dream she had about Hebrews 11:1, where she was praying and people she loved were being transported to where she was. The dream revealed that as she held them in her heart, they were transported—illustrating how faith creates a realm where Heaven responds to our trust in Jesus.

This heavenly realm is compelled to move on our behalf when we exercise faith. Like gravity, it can't help but respond to our faith in Jesus. Faith is the foundation for moving Heaven's economy to Earth.

"All that matters now is living in the faith that works and expresses itself through love." —Galatians 5:6 (TPT)

BECOMING MODERN-DAY HEROES OF FAITH

Today, we stand as inheritors of this great faith legacy. The same God who worked through ancient heroes works through us now. We have even greater access to the Kingdom through Christ and the indwelling Holy Spirit.

As we step into our identity as Heaven's citizens, we become part of this unfolding faith story—modern-day heroes demonstrating God's Kingdom's power and reality in our generation.

The invitation before us is clear: Will we, like those before us, live with faith that fastens onto God's promises and pulls them into reality? Will we walk as though seated with Christ in heavenly places, bringing Heaven's authority, peace, and power into our circumstances?

Let's move forward with the bold, unshakable faith of God revealed in Enoch, David, Elisha, and countless others, knowing the same God who worked through them works through us.

✦ ASCENSION ACTIVATION: PULLING HEAVEN'S REALITY INTO YOUR NOW ✦

This practical exercise will help you begin manifesting heavenly realities in your everyday life:

1. Identify a Need: Choose one area of your life where you need to see Heaven's reality manifest—perhaps healing, provision, wisdom, or breakthrough.

2. Find the Promises: Research 5-3 scriptures that reveal God's promises concerning this area. Write them down where you'll see them daily.

3. Declare Present Reality: Begin declaring these promises as present realities, not future possibilities. For example, instead of "God will provide," say "God is my provider, and I have everything I need" (Philippians 4:19, NIV).

4. Ask for Faith Steps: In prayer, ask the Holy Spirit, "What faith step can I take to pull this heavenly reality into my present circumstances?" Be prepared to act on what you hear.

5. Share Your Journey: Tell others what you're believing in and the steps you're taking. Your testimony will inspire their faith, and their encouragement will strengthen yours.

Remember Jesus' words: "According to your faith let it be done to you" (Matthew 9:29, NIV). Your faith bridges Heaven's realities to your earthly experience, making the invisible visible and bringing the future into now.

☺ Reflection Questions:

? What might you have access to now through faith that you haven't fully realized?

? How can you, like the heroes of faith, draw on Heaven's limitless resources to transform your present circumstances?

? What would happen if you began to declare, by faith, the realities of God's Kingdom over your life, family, and world?

"The true miracle of faith is not that it moves mountains, but that it transforms lives according to the pattern of heaven."—Gregory of Nyssa (*Life of Moses*, 4th century, Book II.121)

Like a child who picks up a towel as a cape and truly believes they can fly, the heroes of faith weren't limited by what their eyes could see—they were empowered by what their spirits could perceive. They didn't just read about heavenly possibilities; they lived as though those possibilities were their present inheritance. And now, that same inheritance is yours.

Will you claim it?

CHAPTER 9: 🔥 CORPORATE ASCENSION TESTIMONIES

🚨 WARNING: This Chapter Contains Contagious
Kingdom Encounters 🚨

Proceed with tissues in hand (spontaneous tears of joy may occur)!

Potential side effects include: ✅ Finding yourself believing that your ordinary prayer gathering could turn extraordinary ✅ Developing unreasonable expectations for your next group Bible study ✅ Experiencing sudden urges to invite friends over for "casual ascension" ✅ Uncontrollable desire to start journaling every spiritual impression

❓ Have you ever noticed how differently people act at a concert versus listening to the same music alone in their car?

There's something about shared experience that amplifies everything—the emotions run higher, the energy feels stronger, and moments become more memorable. The same principle applies to spiritual experiences. When we ascend together, Heaven's realities don't just add up—they multiply exponentially, creating a spiritual atmosphere where even the most skeptical hearts can suddenly perceive what they've been missing all along.

HEAVEN BREAKING INTO EARTH: THE POWER OF TESTIMONY

Every testimony is a living encounter with the Kingdom of God breaking into our world. It's through our personal stories of divine intervention, miraculous breakthroughs, and supernatural encounters that we can see the hand of God moving in the present. My own life is a testament to these Kingdom realities—filled with moments where God's power became evident and His promises came alive. Each encounter has awakened me to His faith but also allowed others to enter into their own experience of God's miraculous power.

In this chapter, I want to share testimonies of how God has moved in my life and in the lives of others. These stories are windows into the Kingdom—testimonies of ascension where we, like those in Isaiah's vision, go up to the mountain of the Lord and learn His ways, walking in His paths. Through these encounters, we experience the reality of being seated with Christ, learning to bring the realities of Heaven into every area of our lives.

"One person's breakthrough becomes everyone's possibility."

THE POWER OF SHARED EXPERIENCE

When believers come together with the intention to ascend, something extraordinary happens. The collective faith creates an atmosphere where Heaven's realities become more tangible, and individual break-throughs multiply into corporate transformation.

This principle of experiencing God's presence more powerfully in community isn't new or experimental—it reflects the consistent pattern we see throughout Scripture. When Solomon dedicated the temple, the glory of God fell so powerfully that the priests couldn't stand (2 Chronicles 5:13-14). At Pentecost, the disciples were "all together in one place" when the Holy Spirit came (Acts 2:1-4). Even Jesus emphasized the special nature of corporate worship when He said, "Where two or three gather in my name, there am I with them" (Matthew 18:20). Throughout church history, from the Celtic prayer circles of St. Patrick's era to the Moravian prayer meetings that sparked global revival, Christians have discovered that something uniquely powerful happens when believers unite their hearts in seeking God's presence. What we're exploring is simply a recovery of this ancient Christian understanding.

This principle of corporate spiritual experience has deep roots in Christian tradition. As Symeon the New Theologian (949-1022 AD) wrote, "When brothers dwell together in unity of heart and purpose, the Holy Spirit flows more freely among them, for they create a dwelling place for God" (*Ethical Discourses*, Discourse 3). Throughout Christian history, monastic communities, prayer gatherings, and spiritual revivals have demonstrated how shared spiritual focus intensifies divine encounter.

ASCENSION IN COMMUNITY: CREATING SPIRITUAL MOMENTUM

🔥 Faith builds upon faith: When one person experiences breakthrough, it creates a pathway for others

🔥 Unity amplifies spiritual sensitivity: Corporate gatherings heighten our awareness of God's presence

🔥 Confirmation strengthens belief: When multiple people witness the same things in the spirit, it builds confidence

The Desert Fathers understood this principle well. Abba Anthony taught that "Our life and our death is with our neighbor" (*Sayings of the Desert Fathers*, 5th century). Spiritual experiences deepened when shared within a community. Similarly, Teresa of Ávila observed that certain graces were specifically granted in community settings that weren't available to hermits in isolation (*The Interior Castle*, 1577, Sixth Mansion).

TESTIMONY OF A KINGDOM ENCOUNTER

Growing in Discernment: Learning to Walk in Heavenly Realities

With every encounter, we are learning and growing. Though we may feel like infants learning to walk in these spiritual realities, someday we will be running!

The 4th-century desert monk Evagrius Ponticus taught about this progressive development of spiritual discernment: "First comes purification, then illumination, and finally, the eyes of the soul open to divine realities" (*Praktikos*, Chapter 1). Similarly, John of the Cross described the spiritual journey as beginning with "stammering" in prayer before growing into maturity in divine communication (*Living Flame of Love*, Stanza 1).

There have been so many fun and meaningful confirmations from the Lord during our prayer times, each one reminding us of how present and involved God is in our lives. One time, at the end of a prayer session, I had a clear vision of Jesus gently kissing each of us on the forehead. It was such a beautiful and intimate moment. Right after, another member of the prayer team, without knowing what I had seen, shared that she saw Jesus doing the exact same thing—giving each of us a kiss on the forehead. These little confirmations are always so fun, but they also carry a deep sense of God's love and affirmation.

The Heart in His Hands: Protection Through Fire

Another powerful confirmation came during a time of intense fire and suffering in my life. Throughout those challenging years, I repeatedly had a vision of Jesus holding my heart in His hands. The image was so vivid, bringing comfort in the midst of incredible pain.

Years later, I was on a call with a prophetic prayer team who didn't know me or my story. At the end of the call, one of the men said, "I saw Jesus holding your heart in His hands. Over the last few years, the enemy came at you, trying to destroy you, but Jesus protected your heart. He turned the enemy's fire into a kiln, using it to mold and shape you for His purpose."

It was such a profound moment, a reminder that even in our darkest seasons, Jesus holds us close, using every trial for our good. The confirmation wasn't just about the vision I had years ago but also about God's unwavering faithfulness through it all. It's easy to discount things of the Spirit, but when God puts an exclamation mark on it, it's incredible to behold!

This confirms what Julian of Norwich (1343-1416 AD) experienced during her own suffering. She wrote, "He did not say, 'You shall not be tempestuous-tossed, you shall not be work-weary, you shall not be discomforted.' But He said, 'You shall not be overcome'" (*Revelations of Divine Love*, Chapter 68). Like many mystics throughout church history, Julian discovered that suffering often becomes the context for our deepest spiritual revelations.

Ascension Activation: Protected Heart

1. Find a quiet place and take a few deep breaths, releasing tension and distractions.

2. Close your eyes and imagine your heart—the center of your emotions, desires, and deepest concerns.

3. Now picture Jesus gently taking your heart into His hands. Feel the warmth, security, and perfect care He provides.

4. If there are areas of pain, disappointment, or wounding in your heart, see Jesus tenderly healing those places with His touch.

5. Hear Him say, "I hold your heart, protecting it from what would harm you, transforming the fires of life into refining moments."

6. Rest in this truth for several minutes, allowing His peace to fill you.

7. Thank Him for His protection and care for the most vulnerable parts of your being.

This exercise draws from the tradition of Ignatian contemplation, developed by Ignatius of Loyola (1491-1556 AD), who taught believers to engage their sanctified imagination in prayer, placing themselves within sacred scenes and dialoguing with Christ. As Teresa of Ávila noted, "The important thing is not to think much but to love much; and so do that which best stirs you to love" (*The Interior Castle*, Fourth Mansion, Chapter 1).

WHEN ASCENSION BREAKS OUT: A CONFERENCE TESTIMONY

Breakout Session Turned into an Ascension Breakout

Once, we were asked to lead a conference breakout session on "Ruling and Reigning with Christ" at the Kingdom Builders Forum. Chantal, our prayer team leader, and I decided not to over-prepare, opting instead for an open discussion, which aligned with our usual approach. We had a one-hour slot for this session.

The conversation during the session was rich, focusing on how we approach prayer, the kingdom, legislation, and governance. After about thirty minutes, I asked my daughter, Bryn, to share her experience of prayer and worship coming from the place of intimacy and engaging with the heart of Jesus, which created a bridge of faith for others to take for what was ahead.

About an hour into the discussion, as we began talking about the Holy Spirit, I sensed the Holy Spirit prompting us to delve into deeper spiritual matters. This naturally led us to discuss Ascension. I then invited Chantal to share her spiritual experiences, dreams, and our team's practices.

One attendee asked if we could engage in Ascension right then, and Chantal and I agreed. Chantal laid the groundwork, and as soon as the Ascension process began, I saw a vision of an angel standing beside her, dressed in mountain climbing gear—a curious sight that initially didn't make much sense to me.

However, the vision continued to unfold, showing Mount Zion and many angels with climbing equipment, passing ropes down to the people in the room. As people ascended, aided by the angels, they reached a part of the mountain covered in beautiful white snow and began "slaloming" up the hill on skis.

This vision resonates with Isaiah's prophecy (Isaiah 2:2-3): "In the last days, the mountain of the Lord's temple will be established... Many peoples will come and say, 'Come, let us go up to the mountain of the Lord'" (NIV). Throughout Christian mystical tradition, the ascent of the holy mountain has been a central metaphor for spiritual progress, as seen in John of the Cross's "Ascent of Mount Carmel" and Gregory of Nyssa's "Life of Moses," where he interprets Moses' ascent of Mount Sinai as the soul's journey into the "divine darkness" of God's presence (*The Life of Moses*, Book II.152-170).

Prophetic Confirmation: The Orange and Purple Climbing Gear

Amazingly, all twenty-five people in the room, most of whom had never experienced Ascension before, participated in the experience. The atmosphere became filled with angelic-like singing from one of the ladies present.

I hesitated to share my vision of the angel in mountain climbing gear (the vision I share in chapter 6) standing beside Chantal, as it seemed so unusual, but when I did, Chantal immediately recognized it from a dream she had in 2022. In that dream, I had given her orange and purple mountain climbing gear, symbolizing preparation for entering the realm of Ascension.

This moment at the conference became a public manifestation of that vision, as God was clearly inviting His people to ascend to heavenly places, co-seated with Christ. It was a powerful "this is that" moment for everyone present.

The session, originally scheduled for one hour, extended to two and a half hours, causing us to miss the scheduled dinner and the entire next session of the conference, but the Holy Spirit was calling the shots! The experience was filled with joy, inner healing, blessing, and a deep sense of intimacy. The only reason we stopped was that someone came looking for their wife, concerned because twenty-five people were missing from the ongoing conference. The session concluded with a sense of divine orchestration, as prayer, healing, and the Spirit moved powerfully among us.

Kingdom Principle: When we create space for the Holy Spirit to move, He often exceeds our expectations and schedules, drawing us into deeper encounters than we could have planned.

This principle has been observed throughout church history during times of revival and spiritual outpouring. The Welsh Revival of 1904-1905 saw services extending far beyond their scheduled times as the Holy Spirit moved. As Evan Roberts, a key figure in that revival, noted, "God's clock is not synchronized with man's timetables" (*The Welsh Revival*, 1905, p. 48).

TRANSFORMATIONAL TESTIMONIES: EXPERIENCING ASCENSION FOR THE FIRST TIME

Bryn's Experience: Enveloped in Divine Love

During a corporate ascension at a Kingdom Builders Forum, my daughter, Bryn, experienced the overwhelming love of God in a tangible way. As she surrendered to the Lord, she encountered waves of His presence and saw visions of His eyes of fire, symbolizing the intensity of His love and His transformative power. This experience marked a turning point in her understanding of ascension, allowing her to engage with God on a deeper level. Here is her experience:

During the breakout session at the conference, Dad asked me to share a bit about the shift that has taken place in my worship and prayer life. I talked about how important it is to engage with the heart of Jesus in everything we do. Without that connection, worship is just singing songs, and prayers are merely words. The power in worship and prayer comes from that deep engagement with Jesus.

If I'm not connected to His heart, then everything I do loses its true power because it's in that connection where transformation happens. The words themselves don't have power; it's the intentionality behind them that brings change.

After sharing this, I was asked to talk about my experience with ascension. Although I had heard a lot about ascension from my dad and Chantal before, it always seemed to go over my head. It wasn't that I didn't understand the idea of it—it was more that I had never fully grasped it until that day.

When we moved into the time to practice ascension together, I thought it was a good opportunity to give it a try. So, I got up from my chair and found a spot in the back of the room where I could be alone with the Lord. I curled up on the floor, wanting space to really focus and be with Him.

As we began, Chantal suggested imagining ourselves being inside a marshmallow, with the marshmallow representing Christ in God. I sat there and started picturing myself as a tiny little chocolate chip, completely enveloped in the marshmallow. A chocolate chip can't move or make choices—it's just there, nestled securely.

That image really resonated with me. It was as though I realized, in that moment, that I couldn't be moved from my place with God. Nothing and no one could take me away from remaining in Christ, in God, enveloped by my little marshmallow of security and love.

Then Chantal encouraged us to ask God to hug us from the inside. At first, it sounded a bit strange, but I decided to give it a try. As I asked God to hug me from the inside, I felt the most warm, beautiful, and intense hug I've ever experienced. It was overwhelming in the best way possible.

In my mind, I then asked the Lord, "How do I do this? How do I ascend?" And so clearly, He responded, "You don't have to do anything. Just give me permission." So I surrendered, saying, "Okay, Lord, whatever You want to do, wherever You want to go, I'm here. I give You permission."

As soon as I said that, I started feeling waves washing over me—over my shoulders and head. It was as if a flow of water was cascading over me. The waves became visible in my mind, and then, emerging from behind them, I saw eyes of fire. The eyes were so strong, so bright, and so intense that even now, when I close my eyes and look up, I can still see them as if they've been burned into my vision.

It's kind of amazing that I can only see them when my eyes are closed—when I'm not looking at anything else, just resting in that space with God.

As this was happening, I heard laughter—pure, joyful laughter that I knew was the laughter of Heaven. It was the joy of the Lord, of Heaven rejoicing in our pursuit of Him, in our openness to Him doing new things in and through us.

Then, at one point, a woman in the room began to hum a melody. At first, I thought it was just the sounds of Heaven, but then I realized it was actually someone in the room. Yet, there was this deeper understanding that even though it was a person, it was also the sounds of Heaven—the sounds of angels. I wasn't the only one who felt that; others sensed it too. It was a powerful moment of Heaven touching earth.

That experience in the breakout session was profound, and it's something I'll never forget. It was a beautiful demonstration of how, when we fully engage with the heart of Jesus and surrender to Him, we open ourselves up to the incredible realities of His Kingdom.

Bryn's experience reflects what Catherine of Siena (1347-1380 AD) described as "resting in the cell of self-knowledge"—a place of intimate divine encounter. Catherine wrote, "Build yourself a cell inside your mind, from which you can never flee" (*The Dialogue*, Chapter 4). This inner sanctuary, this space of surrender, becomes the gateway to profound spiritual experience.

☺ Reflection Questions:

? How might you open yourself more fully to the transformative power of God in your life?

? What steps can you take to surrender more deeply and allow God to lead you into new spiritual experiences?

Nick's Experience: The Fire in His Veins

At the same Forum, Nick experienced a breakthrough in prayer as he envisioned running toward Jesus and embracing Him in joy. This encounter not only deepened his relationship with God but also opened the door for him to experience the fire of the Holy Spirit flowing through him in a tangible way. The experience transformed his understanding of ascension and gave him a greater awareness of the Holy Spirit's work in his life.

Here is Nick's experience:

I attended a breakout session with Bryan Elliott, his daughter Bryn, and his company's prayer team leader, Chantal. Bryan and Chantal were discussing the company's prayer format and the mindset during these prayers of "ascension." I was having difficulty grasping the concept.

Bryn explained a form of ascension, regarding her experience with prayer and worship, although ascension was not part of her practice until that day. She put it simply and directly for the group—from a place of intimacy, she visualized a clear and direct connection to God. This wasn't a prayer or experience projected outwardly, but one directed truly upward to Him.

There was something about Bryn's description and conviction that helped me understand and open my mind and heart in a way I didn't even know was possible. Another member of the group suggested we engage in an ascension right then to experience it for ourselves.

Chantal led the group as we each surrendered to God in our own way. She prayed softly throughout the session while others sang or whispered prayers. As I began praying, I envisioned a link between myself and the heavenly realm, imagining what it would look like to be directly connected.

My breakthrough came when I pictured Jesus standing far in the distance. I felt a surge of joy as I started walking, then running, then sprinting toward Him. It was the kind of joy that young children surely feel when they run to their mother or father. I was sprinting toward my Heavenly Father and leapt into His loving arms with an enormous hug.

I was overcome with emotion and replayed the scene over and over. The prayer evolved as my children joined in this embrace with Jesus.

We were lifted off the ground as if we were ascending to Heaven. This part of the prayer was my introduction to ascension.

I briefly came out of prayer to see if the session was complete and was inspired by others who were now crying joyfully, singing, and praying aloud. Knowing that I had more time, I decided to re-enter my prayer. To my amazement, I was almost instantly brought back into the depths of my previous experience.

This time, as I was trying to picture Jesus literally living within my heart, I saw what I felt was the hand of God placed gently on my physical heart. I felt a flood of fire flow through my veins, beginning at my heart and running out through my fingertips. I felt my bowed head lift up, and a flood of blinding light filled my closed eyes. The light was continuous and vibrant, as if I was moving through it at warp speed. I could feel my eyes moving erratically and involuntarily, trying to make sense of it all.

When the prayer ended, I felt a peace and calm I had never experienced. I shared my experience with the group, who responded by surrounding me and praying over me. Bryan spoke a powerful prayer of a father's blessing over me as I felt the energy and love of the group flow in.

Before leaving the conference room, I saw a small group praying over another member of the breakout session. I joined them, placing my hand on this man, and felt the same flood of fire flow through my body, out through my fingertips, and onto him. It felt as if the fire of the Holy Spirit was being shared directly from me after blessing me with the same feeling.

In church the following week, I was deeply moved as we sang "King of My Heart" by Bethel Music, which includes the lyrics about the King of my heart being the fire inside my veins. It was a full-circle moment, realizing that it was indeed the Holy Spirit and the love of God filling my veins with fire.

Since the Kingdom Builder Forum, I have been able to access these sorts of interactions with the Holy Spirit through Ascension on my own. I was amazed to encounter the Holy Spirit in this way because I didn't think I had the depth of faith required to access it. I was wrong. I encourage those from all walks of faith to give themselves a chance to unlock their prayer potential!

Nick's experience parallels what Symeon the New Theologian described as the "baptism of fire"—a tangible experience of the Holy Spirit's presence. Symeon wrote, "For those who have been deemed worthy of becoming children of God...divine fire comes to dwell within them" (*Ethical Discourses*, Discourse 5). Similarly, the Russian saint Seraphim of Sarov (1754-1833 AD) was known to be physically illuminated by divine fire during prayer, teaching that "acquiring the Holy Spirit" was the ultimate aim of Christian life (*Conversation with Motovilov*, 1831).

Mika's Experience: Heaven's Invasion

Recently, I had the opportunity to attend a conference called Kingdom Builders Forum. During one of the breakout sessions led by Bryan Elliott, something truly extraordinary happened. Bryan and Chantal guided us into a group ascension, and it turned out to be one of the most powerful experiences of corporate ascension I've ever encountered. It felt as though everyone in the room ascended together into the heavenly realms, and the atmosphere became saturated with the presence of the Kingdom.

The unity of our ascension created an atmosphere so charged with God's presence that it was undeniable. We weren't just praying or worshiping; we were collectively encountering God in a way that transcended our usual experiences. At one point during the ascension, I could sense the presence of angels in the room, their voices blending into a heavenly chorus. Then a woman in the room began to sing aloud in the natural, what the angels were singing in the Spirit. It was an amazing moment where Heaven and Earth seemed to converge.

As we continued in this ascension, I felt an overwhelming sense of the joy of the Lord. It was so intense that I struggled to contain my laughter, trying not to distract others around me, but the joy just kept bubbling out. The atmosphere was thick with God's glory, and it felt like Heaven had truly invaded our gathering.

When we finally came out of the ascension time, the testimonies that came forth were awesome. People shared how they had been ministered to in deep and personal ways, encountering God's love, healing, and revelation. That one ascension time left a significant impact on everyone involved, and it continues to amaze me how, when we intentionally turn our affection toward Heaven, God responds by pouring out into our earthly realm.

Mika's experience reflects what Bernard of Clairvaux (1090-1153 AD) described as the "ecstasy of devotion" where the soul is "no longer in itself, but caught up to God." Bernard wrote that in such moments, "the soul forgets itself and becomes that which it beholds" (*On the Love of God*, Book IV, Chapter 9). This joyful surrender characterizes authentic spiritual ascension.

⁖ Ascension Activation: Corporate Gathering ⁖

This exercise is designed for a small group setting:

1. Prepare the atmosphere: Begin with soft worship music playing in the background. Have everyone sit comfortably.

2. Center in Christ: Take 2-3 minutes of silence, focusing on Jesus and letting go of distractions.

3. Invite the Holy Spirit: Have one person pray a simple invitation for the Holy Spirit to lead your time together.

4. Visualization prompt: Share Chantal's "marshmallow" imagery or another simple picture that helps people imagine being completely surrounded by and immersed in God's presence.

5.   Permission prayer: Lead the group in a simple prayer of sur-
     render: "Lord, we give you permission to take us wherever You
     want to go in the Spirit. We open ourselves to Your presence
     and Your leading."

6.   Rest in His presence: Allow 10-15 minutes of quiet, where
     each person simply receives from the Lord. Encourage people
     to notice any impressions, images, sensations, or words they
     might receive.

7.   Share experiences: After the quiet time, create space for people
     to share what they experienced. Affirm each person's experi-
     ence without judgment.

8.   Close in gratitude: End by thanking God for His presence and
     what He's revealed.

Remember: The goal isn't to force an experience but to create space
for God to move in each person's heart in His unique way.

This approach draws from the Benedictine tradition of lectio divina—a
contemplative practice of reading, meditation, prayer, and contemplation. As Benedict of Nursia (480—547 AD) taught, "Listen with the ear
of your heart" (*Rule of St. Benedict*, Prologue), emphasizing receptivity
to God's voice rather than striving for spiritual experience.

KINGDOM IMPLICATIONS: WHAT THESE TESTIMONIES TEACH US

Transforming Our Understanding of Prayer

These experiences of ascension transform our understanding of prayer
from a one-way communication to an intimate dialogue and encounter
with God. Prayer becomes less about presenting requests and more
about entering into God's presence, seeing from His perspective, and
being transformed by the encounter.

This shift reflects what the Eastern Orthodox tradition calls "nepsis" or watchfulness—a state of spiritual alertness and receptivity. As Isaac the Syrian wrote, "Enter eagerly into the treasure house that lies within you, and so you will see the treasure house of Heaven: for the two are the same, and there is but one single entry to them both" (*Ascetical Homilies*, Homily 2).

Breaking Religious Mindsets

Many of these testimonies reveal how people broke through religious mindsets and limitations to experience God in fresh, powerful ways. When Nick said, "I was amazed to encounter the Holy Spirit in this way because I didn't think I had the depth of faith required to access it. I was wrong," he captured how many of us unnecessarily limit our expectations of what God will do.

Augustine of Hippo reflected this breakthrough when he wrote, "I have been climbing the heights of Your Word, and now what wonders I see! Too late have I loved You, O Beauty ever ancient, ever new, too late have I loved You!" (*Confessions*, Book X, Chapter 27). His confession captures the moment when religious concepts give way to actual encounters.

The Power of Corporate Ascension

These stories highlight the impact of ascending together. When believers unite in faith and focus, the collective experience creates an atmosphere where Heaven's realities become more accessible to everyone.

As Jesus promised, when two or three gather in His name, His presence is magnified among them (Matthew 18:20, NIV).

This principle is illustrated in the Pentecostal outpouring recorded in Acts 2 (NKJV), where the disciples were "all together in one place" when the Holy Spirit came. Throughout church history, from Celtic prayer circles to Moravian prayer movements to modern revival gatherings, the corporate dimension has accelerated spiritual experience.

Simple Entry Points Lead to Profound Encounters

The testimonies show that entering into ascension doesn't require complex methods or years of spiritual training. Simple visualization tools like Chantal's "marshmallow" imagery provided accessible entry points for people to experience profound encounters with God.

This simplicity reflects Jesus' own teaching that we must become like children to enter the Kingdom (Matthew 18:3, NIV). Teresa of Lisieux (1873-1897 AD) embodied this principle in her "Little Way," teaching that spiritual greatness comes through childlike simplicity rather than complex spiritual techniques (*Story of a Soul,* Chapter 9).

Lasting Transformation, Not Just Momentary Experiences

These weren't just emotional moments that faded. Nick noted that "Since the Kingdom Builder Forum, I have been able to access these sorts of interactions with the Holy Spirit through Ascension on my own." True encounters with God produce lasting change, equipping us to live continuously from a heavenly perspective.

? Wonder Questions:

? After exploring the concept of being a heavenly being with access to the realms of Heaven, how has your vision of what is possible expanded?

? What transformation can you bring into the world through the power and wisdom of God within you?

CHANTAL'S RESPONSE: HIGHER CONSCIOUSNESS, HIGHER IMPACT

"No problem can be solved from the same level of consciousness that created it."—Albert Einstein

The Earth cannot transform the Earth! Only Heaven's realm coming down will transform the Earth back to its original intent! That's why for over 2000 years we have been praying what Jesus told us to pray—that Heaven would be here on earth! We are the gates that Heaven passes through to be released on earth. We are the dispensers of Heaven's realm now!

To ascend in the Lord is to have the mind of Christ, as Scripture teaches in 1 Corinthians 2:16. Every time a saint in history went into divine encounters, there was a dimensional shift, a consciousness shift, the fabric of society was changed, and divine invasion took place to change the timeline of history!

Downloads of technology! Science discoveries! Anointed new songs written! Groundbreaking artwork created!

"The finest emotion of which we are capable is the mystic emotion. Herein lies the root of all art and all true science. Anyone to whom this feeling is alien, who is no longer capable of wonderment and lives in a state of fear is a dead man. To know that what is impenetrable for us really exists and manifests itself as the highest wisdom and the most radiant beauty, whose gross forms alone are intelligible to our poor faculties—this knowledge, this feeling—that is the core of the true religious sentiment. In this sense, and in this sense alone, I rank myself among profoundly religious men."—Albert Einstein

The throne room reality is to allow yourself to be transfigured into the image of the One you behold. As you gaze on Him, you are being transfigured. The goal of this is to bring you into more glory. As we are being glorified, He is being glorified and revealed!

Jesus is the treasure of all the wisdom of all the ages available to us now through our union with Him! And now He lives in you, and you live in Him.

"For our spiritual wealth is in him, like hidden treasure waiting to be discovered—Heaven's wisdom and endless riches of revelation knowledge." —Colossians 2:3 (TPT)

Chantal's perspective resonates deeply with Gregory of Nyssa's concept of spiritual transformation: "The soul, beholding the beauty of the Beloved, is constantly being transformed into that which it beholds" (*On Spiritual Perfection*, 4th century). Similarly, Paul's declaration that "we all, with unveiled face, beholding the glory of the Lord, are being transformed into the same image from one degree of glory to another" (2 Corinthians 3:18, NIV) captures this transformative contemplation.

PRACTICAL STEPS FOR DEVELOPING ASCENSION IN YOUR LIFE

1. *Start with Stillness:* Begin by creating intentional times of stillness each day. Even 5-10 minutes of focused quiet, away from distractions, can create space for your spirit to become more aware of heavenly realities.

This practice of stillness has deep roots in Christian tradition. The Desert Fathers spoke of hesychia—sacred stillness—as the foundation of spiritual experience. As Abba Moses taught a young monk, "Go, sit in your cell, and your cell will teach you everything" (*Sayings of the Desert Fathers*, 5th century).

2. *Practice Holy Imagination:* God often speaks through sanctified imagination. Try simple visualization exercises like picturing yourself seated with Christ in heavenly places (Ephesians 2:6, NKJV, NIV) or imagining Jesus standing before you.

Ignatius of Loyola developed this approach in his Spiritual Exercises, teaching believers to use their imagination to enter biblical scenes and engage with Jesus. As he wrote, "It is not knowing much, but realizing and relishing things interiorly, that contents and satisfies the soul" (*Spiritual Exercises*, 16th century, Second Week).

3. *Develop Spiritual Sensitivity Through Worship:* Worship shifts our focus from earthly concerns to heavenly realities. Make worship a daily practice, not just singing songs but truly engaging your heart with Jesus.

Throughout Christian history, worship has been recognized as a gateway to spiritual experience. David's worship enabled him to access prophetic revelation, and the early church understood worship as entering God's courts. As Evagrius Ponticus taught, "If you are a theologian, you will pray truly; and if you pray truly, you are a theologian" (*On Prayer*, 4th century, Chapter 61).

4. *Keep a Heavenly Encounters Journal:* Record your experiences, impressions, and dreams. This builds faith as you look back and see patterns of how God has been speaking to you.

The practice of spiritual journaling has precedent in the Desert Fathers' collections of sayings and Teresa of Ávila's detailed accounts of her interior experiences. As Julian of Norwich meticulously recorded her "showings," she created a record that has blessed generations of believers seeking deeper communion with God (*Revelations of Divine Love,* 14th century).

5. *Join with Others:* Find people who are also pursuing deeper encounters with God. Corporate ascension often accelerates individual growth and provides confirmation and encouragement.

The Celtic Christians understood this principle with their concept of "soul friends" (anam cara), companions on the spiritual journey who help us discern and deepen our experience of God. As Brigid of Kildare reportedly said, "A person without a soul friend is like a body without a head" *(The Life of St. Brigid,* 7th century).

6. *Trust the Process:* Remember that ascension is not about performance but permission. As Bryn learned, you don't have to "do" anything; you simply give God permission to lead you.

This aligns with Brother Lawrence's teaching on the "practice of the presence of God," where he emphasized receptivity over achievement. As he wrote, "We should establish ourselves in a sense of God's Presence by continually conversing with Him... not in studied terms of mystical prayer, but with words of love flowing spontaneously from the heart" (*The Practice of the Presence of God,* 17th century, Fourth Conversation).

THE INVITATION STANDS

These testimonies are more than interesting stories—they are invitations. They reveal that heavenly encounters are available to everyone who is willing to open their heart and give God permission to lead them into deeper experiences of His presence.

? **Wonder Questions:**

? What if the veil between Heaven and earth is thinner than you've been taught to believe?

? What if Jesus is inviting you, right now, to ascend and see from His perspective?

? What if your next prayer time could be more than words—it could be an encounter that transforms how you see everything?

The invitation to ascend is not reserved for the spiritual elite or those with decades of prayer experience. It's extended to every believer who is willing to say, "Yes, Lord, take me where You want me to go."

The church father Irenaeus wrote, "The glory of God is a human being fully alive" (*Against Heresies,* 2nd century, Book IV, Chapter 20). Perhaps becoming fully alive means awakening to the heavenly realities that have always surrounded us, stepping into the ascended life that is our inheritance in Christ.

❖ Final Reflection Questions:

? What one step can you take today to begin experiencing the reality of ascension in your own life?

? How might saying "yes" to this invitation change not only your spiritual experience but also how you impact the world around you?

As Catherine of Siena so beautifully expressed, "Be who God meant you to be and you will set the world on fire" (*Letters,* 14th century, Letter T273). The world is waiting for believers who have truly awakened to who they are in Christ, who live from their seated position with Him, and who bring Heaven's realities into every situation they encounter.

As I love food, here is a closing analogy. Think of sharing your first ascension experience like the moment when someone tastes truly authentic cuisine from another culture for the first time. You can describe ingredients and cooking methods all day long, but that first bite creates an "Aha!" moment no words could convey. Your testimony becomes the invitation that helps others discover what they've been missing—a taste of Heaven that changes everything.

The doorway is open. The Spirit is calling. Heaven is waiting.

Will you step in?

"The more we ascend to God, the more we descend in love toward our neighbor, and the veil between Heaven and earth grows ever thinner until, in moments of grace, it seems not to exist at all."——Gregory the Great (*Pastoral Rule,* 6th century, Part III, Chapter 17)

EPILOGUE: THE ASCENDED LIFE—
YOUR INVITATION TO RISE

⚠ WARNING: These Final Pages May Forever
Change Your Reality ⚠

Proceed with your heart wide open (the adventure of your life-time awaits)!

Potential side effects include: ✅ Developing an unquenchable hunger for heavenly realities ✅ Finding it impossible to return to "normal" Christianity ✅ Seeing divine possibilities where others see dead ends ✅ Spontaneously becoming a gateway for Heaven's invasion of Earth

Picture standing at the edge of an undiscovered country, knowing that just beyond the threshold lies everything you've ever longed for. The air tingles with expectation; you can almost taste the adventure. Your heart races not with fear but with anticipation—this is the moment everything changes. That's what the ascended life feels like—the exhilarating recognition that the greatest journey of your life isn't behind you. It hasn't even begun.

What if your greatest adventure with God hasn't even begun?

"I have been ascending and descending in the Spirit for more than forty years now. When you learn to be caught up in a moment, in the twinkling of an eye, you can see all the things that were, all the things that are, and all the things that are yet to come... It is so magnificent, so majestic, so overwhelming to have been given the privilege to see the dynamic unfolding of Yahweh's sovereign plan for mankind."——Nancy Cohen (*Heavenly Encounters,* 2019, p. 147)

THE CALL TO ASCEND: AN INVITATION FOR EVERYONE

The ascended life is both mystical experience and practical reality—an invitation to live as citizens of Heaven while walking on earth. This call isn't limited to spiritual elites or those with decades of prayer experience. It's extended to every believer, including you!

Throughout history, from Desert Fathers to medieval mystics to modern believers, this invitation has remained open. As we align with Heaven's perspective, we begin to walk in Christ's authority, bringing Heaven's solutions into our earthly circumstances.

The practice of ascension becomes a powerful tool for:

⁚ Deepening intimacy with God—not by striving toward Him but by awakening to His constant presence

⁚ Accessing divine wisdom—tapping into understanding that transcends human limitations

⁚ Walking in the Spirit's power—operating from rest rather than religious effort

⁚ Transforming circumstances—bringing Heaven's reality into every situation we face

Whether through personal prayer or corporate gatherings, we're called to ascend into heavenly realms and live from God's Kingdom reality—not as a distant hope but as our present inheritance. We're not climbing up to reach Heaven; we're awakening to our position already seated there with Christ!

This journey isn't about arriving somewhere new—it's about recognizing where you've always been in Christ.

FROM SERVANTS TO FRIENDS: LIVING IN DIVINE PARTNERSHIP

Through our union with Christ, we're seated in heavenly places, called to live from this position of authority and intimacy with God. As Jesus declared:

"I have never called you 'servants,' because a master doesn't confide in his servants, and servants don't always understand what the master is doing. But I call you my most intimate friends, for I reveal to you everything that I've heard from my Father." —John 15:15 (TPT)

This elevation from servants to friends marks a profound shift in our relationship with God. As His friends, we share His heart and plans. We're invited into divine partnership, bringing Heaven's blueprints to Earth and participating in His Kingdom's unfolding.

The distinction is crucial: servants work to earn approval, but friends operate from established love and trust. Servants wait for instructions, but friends participate in the creative process. This is the essence of the ascended life—stepping into the fullness of friendship with God, where we don't just do His work; we share His heart.

Saint Augustine captured this beautifully: "God thirsts to be thirsted for" (*Confessions,* 5th century, Book XIII.8). Our relationship with Him isn't a distant obligation but an intimate desire.

Through ascension, we experience communion not as a future reward but as our present reality. We are already in Christ, and Christ is already in us. The veil that once seemed to separate Heaven and earth has been torn, and we're invited to live in the fullness of this unveiled relationship.

STEPPING INTO HEAVENLY REALMS: YOUR PRACTICAL PATH

Ascension is not simply about experiencing Heaven one day—it's about waking up to where you already are right now. It's a shift from seeking distant encounters to recognizing your present reality in Christ. Jesus lived in both the heavenly and earthly realms simultaneously (John 3:13, NIV), and He invites us to do the same. The more we intentionally engage Heaven, the more powerfully we manifest its reality on Earth.

"He raised us up with Christ the exalted One, *and we ascended with him into the glorious perfection and authority* of the heavenly realm, for we are now co-seated as one with Christ!" — Ephesians 2:6 (TPT)

A SEVEN-STEP GUIDE TO ENGAGING ASCENSION

Each step in this process builds on the previous one, helping you cultivate a continuous awareness of your heavenly citizenship:

Step 1: Prepare Your Heart and Mind

Before ascending, shift your focus from earthly distractions to heavenly realities through silence and intentionality.

Practical Action:

- Find a quiet place, take a few deep breaths, and say aloud:
- "I am already in the heavenly places. My spirit is fully alive in Christ."

Step 2: Step into the Reality of God's Presence

The door to the Most Holy Place is open because of Christ's finished work. Boldly enter God's throne room.

Practical Action:

- Close your eyes and envision yourself standing before God's throne. Declare:
- "I ascend into Your presence, fully awake in my spirit."

Step 3: Engage Your Spiritual Senses

You have spiritual senses to perceive and interact with heavenly realms. The more you exercise them, the clearer they become.

Practical Action:

- Ask the Holy Spirit to open your spiritual eyes and ears. Imagine Jesus approaching you—observe, listen, feel. Record what you sense.

Step 4: Encounter Jesus as Your Guide

Jesus desires to guide your spiritual encounters. Trust Him as He reveals His Kingdom and leads you deeper.

Practical Action:

- Ask: "Jesus, where do You want to take me today?"
- Trust the impressions, images, or directions you receive.

Step 5: Receive Kingdom Assignments from Heaven's Courts

You have a unique destiny written in Heaven. Engage the courts of Heaven to discover your divine mandates.

Practical Action:

- Declare confidently: "Father, what is written about me in my scrolls?"
- Record new insights or instructions.

Step 6: Receive Heavenly Blueprints and Strategies

Heaven has answers to every earthly challenge. Seek divine blueprints for daily living.

Practical Action:

- Ask: "Father, what are You doing today that I can partner with?"
- Receive divine inspiration and act upon it.

Step 7: Descend with Kingdom Authority

You are designed to be a gateway between Heaven and Earth, manifesting heavenly realities in everyday life.

Practical Action:

- Declare daily: "I carry the presence of Heaven wherever I go."
- Bring heavenly peace, healing, and solutions into your circumstances.

THE KINGDOM NOW: HEAVEN WITHIN REACH

As we conclude this journey together, remember that the Kingdom of God isn't merely a concept to read about or a future to await—it's a present reality to live in now. The Kingdom isn't confined to:

◆ The pages of Scripture—it's the living Word manifesting through you

◆ The walls of a church—it's God's presence transforming every environment

◆ A distant future beyond death—it's resurrection life available today

Instead, it's within you, expanding around you, and waiting to be unveiled in your:

◆ Personal life and relationships—transforming how you love and connect with others

◆ Family and community—bringing divine order and Kingdom culture

◆ Workplace and influence—releasing supernatural solutions and wisdom

◆ Creative expressions—manifesting Heaven's design in tangible form

Jesus was emphatic: "The kingdom of God is already within you!" (Luke 17:21, TPT). This wasn't a metaphor or future promise—it was a proclamation of present truth. The Kingdom isn't coming someday; it's here now, breaking forth through those who recognize their position in Christ.

LIVING IN THE DIVINE TENSION

Throughout this book, we've explored the "now and not yet"—while we await God's Kingdom's full manifestation, we're already living in its unfolding. In this divine tension, we discover our greatest authority and purpose.

Through our union with Jesus, we have the power to pull Heaven's promises into our present, empowered to:

✳ Live beyond earthly limitations—drawing on divine resources rather than human strength

✳ Bring healing where there is pain—releasing Heaven's wholeness into broken situations

✳ Establish peace where there is chaos—carrying God's presence as an atmosphere

⭐ Shine light where there is darkness—revealing truth that dispels every deception

Our faith becomes the bridge between seen and unseen, allowing Heaven's realities to invade earth. As Brad Jersak says, "The Kingdom is like the sunrise—dawn has broken, but full daylight is still unfolding" (*A More Christlike Way,* 2019, p. 201). We live in this divine tension, celebrating what has already come while eagerly anticipating what's still being revealed.

LIVING THE ASCENDED LIFE DAILY

Ascension isn't an occasional spiritual experience—it's your daily reality in Christ. Each day, begin from your heavenly seat, live from a continual awareness of God's presence, and become a walking portal of Heaven's realities.

Daily Ascension Declaration:

"I am co-seated with Christ in the heavenly realm. My mind is fixed on eternal realities. I walk in revelation knowledge, receiving heavenly blueprints daily.

Everywhere I go, I release Heaven into Earth."

CHANTAL'S JOY: LIVING AS HEAVEN'S GOVERNMENT ON EARTH

You know you've been transported to another dimension when you see things you have no words for! When sharing these experiences, you must dig deep into human language to express what you saw.

I have been both fascinated and mortified during heavenly encounters! I've fearfully trembled in awe and wonder trying to make sense of things I saw or experienced! All this has changed how I pray, knowing that through the Holy Spirit's power, I get to participate in the restoration of all things, starting NOW!

One of my most powerful dreams revealed the divine potential within each believer. God showed me the power of life within me to co-create and bring restoration to His creation. He revealed that everything He created already contains the seed of its original intent—its perfect design before the fall.

This seed of divine purpose waits within creation for believers who, through the frequency of joy and God's life-breath within them, can call forth life as He intended from the beginning. This transformed how I see my role in the world.

We're not trying to create something new—we're awakening to what has always been God's design. Through our union with Christ, we partner with Him to unveil and restore what was hidden but never lost.

In Christ, we've been given authority to participate in ruling and reigning with Him over creation. This was always His intention—that we would:

Co-create with divine inspiration—bringing Heaven's patterns into earthly expression

Co-labor with heavenly wisdom—solving problems from above rather than below

Co-rule with Kingdom authority—establishing God's righteous order in every sphere

As I shared earlier, I remember standing by the ocean praying when the Lord interrupted me with a question that changed everything:

"Where is my government right now?"

I hesitantly answered, "I guess right here... is it me?"

He confirmed, "Yes, you are my government touching the ground. Would you like to legislate over My creation because My government needs to be activated right here?"

Overwhelmed by the invitation, I wondered, "Am I able to do that?"

His response still resonates: "You never do anything alone; you're always inside of Me and with Me."

From that moment, it has been my joy to stand on ocean shores and release God's shalom, blessing, restoration, and pleasure from Heaven's realm over the ocean!

This divine invitation to participate in Heaven's government isn't about achieving a position—it's about awakening to where we're already seated. "We don't ascend to get authority; we ascend because we already have it." Our ascension isn't creating a new reality; it's recognizing the reality that has always existed in Christ.

There's never a dull moment with God! Life union with God is never boring! Our journey isn't meant to look like typical Sunday services. We're not locals on this planet—we're a mystical body, the Church, functioning as God's government!

YOUR FIRST STEP HIGHER: A SIMPLE DAILY ACTIVATION

Before closing this book, take a moment to engage in this simple ascension activation:

1. Find a quiet space where you won't be interrupted for 5-10 minutes

2. Close your eyes and take three deep breaths, releasing any tension or distractions

3. Picture yourself seated with Christ in heavenly places (Ephesians 2:6, NKJV, NIV) — don't strain or force this, simply rest in the awareness that this is already your position

4. Ask the Holy Spirit, "Show me what it means to live from this heavenly position"

5. Rest in His presence, noticing any impressions, images, or thoughts that come to mind

6. Write down what you experienced, even if it seems simple or small

7. Take one step of obedience based on what you received

This simple practice can become a daily rhythm that trains your spirit to ascend and your mind to think from Heaven's perspective. As you continue this journey, ascension becomes less of an event and more of a lifestyle—a constant awareness of your heavenly position and authority in Christ.

Remember, ascension isn't about creating a new reality; it's about awakening to what has always been true. You don't need to strive for this experience—simply rest in Christ's finished work and allow your consciousness to align with your true position in Him.

FROM KNOWLEDGE TO ACTIVATION

All our understanding of God's Kingdom ultimately comes down to one thing: activation. It's not enough to know about the Kingdom or even experience its power momentarily—we're called to live it out, bringing Heaven's reality to Earth through:

💪 Faith that sees beyond natural limitations—recognizing what's already true in Christ

Action that demonstrates Kingdom authority—moving with Heaven's confidence

Bold obedience that releases divine transformation—partnering with God's purposes

You were created for more than just survival; you were designed to thrive in the Holy Spirit's power and bring transformation to the world around you. The time to ascend is now—Heaven is at hand, and you're called to be an active participant in God's divine plan.

THE PATH FORWARD: RISING HIGHER

As you close this book, my prayer is that you'll continue seeking God's Kingdom's fullness in your life. Let this be just the beginning—a starting point for:

Deeper intimacy with Jesus—knowing Him not just as Savior but as friend, partner, and Lord

Greater faith in His promises—living from what He has already accomplished

Bolder living from Heaven's limitless reality—manifesting Kingdom culture wherever you go

May you rise higher, engage with heavenly realms, and experience God's Kingdom power here and now. Remember, the invitation to ascend is always open, and Jesus continues saying, "Come up here."

Think of it this way: when a butterfly emerges from its chrysalis, it doesn't need to be taught to fly—it simply awakens to the wings it's always had. In the same way, your ascension isn't about developing new abilities but awakening to the heavenly reality that has always been your true home. The veil has been torn, the door stands open, and Jesus extends His hand.

This ascended life isn't a distant goal but your birthright in Christ. Your ascension begins with a simple shift in awareness—recognizing who you already are in Him and where you're already positioned in heavenly realms.

The invitation to ascend remains open.

Will you go up?

"Heaven is not a place and earth is not a place. They are states of consciousness that vibrate at different frequencies. As you learn to attune yourself to the higher frequencies of the Spirit, heaven and earth become one in your experience."—Macarius the Great (*Spiritual Homilies,* 4th century, Homily 5)

GLOSSARY

Ain Soph Aur- Hebrew term meaning "Endless Light," describing the infinite, uncreated radiance of God. It represents the boundless divine presence that fills all things and the pure essence of God's being beyond time and space. This concept is deeply connected to ascension as we step into the light of divine reality. (Colossians 2:3)

Aliyah- Hebrew word meaning "to go up" or "to ascend." In ancient Israel, making Aliyah meant traveling to Jerusalem for sacred feasts. In our spiritual journey, it symbolizes our ascent into higher realms of God's presence, transcending earthly limitations to experience divine reality. (Isaiah 2:3)

Ascension- The practice of living from our seated position in Christ—accessing and experiencing heavenly realities while still on earth. Not about leaving our bodies or escaping the physical world, but aligning our awareness with our true spiritual position. Ascension is awakening to where we already are in Christ. (Ephesians 2:6, NKJV; Colossians 3:1-2)

Bi-locational Reality- Our capacity to exist and function in both heavenly and earthly realms simultaneously. Through our union with Christ, we can operate in multiple dimensions at once, with our spirit engaged in heavenly places while our body remains on earth. (John 3:13; Ephesians 2:6, NKJV)

Contemplative Prayer- The practice of quiet stillness and simple attention to God's presence. Unlike prayer filled with speaking and requesting, contemplative prayer invites us into profound silence before God, recognizing that we are already seated with Christ in heavenly places. (Psalm 46:10)

Co-seated- The reality of being positioned with Christ in heavenly places, sharing in His authority, perspective, and access to the Father. This is not a future hope but our present inheritance through our union with Jesus. (Ephesians 2:6, NKJV)

Divine Pattern Recognition- The ability to perceive God's orchestration unfolding in our lives, connecting past revelations with present circumstances. It's seeing reality as it truly is: infused with God's presence and purpose, recognizing His fingerprints in seeming "coincidences." (Deuteronomy 19:15)

Ekklesia- More than just a church gathering, the Ekklesia is a governing body of believers executing Heaven's will on Earth. In its original context, it referred to a legislative assembly with authority to establish governance and order in society. Through Christ, believers are empowered to function as Heaven's government on earth. (Matthew 16:18-19)

Heavenly Realms- The spiritual dimensions that exist beyond natural perception, where divine realities and beings operate. These realms aren't distant or separate from us but interpenetrate our physical reality and are accessible through our spirit's awareness. (Ephesians 1:3, 2:6, 3:10)

Jacob's Ladder- The symbolic connection between Heaven and Earth, represented in Jacob's dream of a ladder with angels ascending and descending (Genesis 28:12). Through Christ, believers become living Jacob's ladders—gateways for heavenly activity to flow into earthly circumstances. (John 1:51)

King-Priest Identity- Our dual function of ruling with authority (kings) while ministering to God in intimate worship and communion (priests). This identity, foreshadowed by Melchizedek in the Old Testament, enables us to operate in both authority and intimacy simultaneously. (Revelation 1:6; 1 Peter 2:9)

Kingdom Intelligence- Supernatural insight and wisdom received from Heaven for earthly application. More than human wisdom or intellectual understanding, it's divine revelation that provides solutions, strategies, and understanding beyond natural capacity. (1 Corinthians 2:9-10)

Metanoia- Far more than "repentance" or "changing your mind," metanoia is a radical transformation of perception that reshapes how we see reality. A spiritual awakening that flows from spirit to mind rather than mind to spirit, empowering us to discern God's will and live from His perspective. (Romans 12:2)

Ruach- Hebrew word for "spirit," conveying both breath and divine life force. Your spirit knows truth instinctively without analysis, functioning as the true essence of who you are in Christ. (Proverbs 20:27)

Sanctified Imagination- The God-given faculty that allows us to perceive spiritual realities beyond physical sight. Not mere fantasy, but a receiving antenna that bridges the gap between your spirit's heavenly position and your mind's earthly experience. When surrendered to the Holy Spirit, imagination becomes a primary way we receive divine impressions, visions, and revelations. (Ephesians 1:18)

Selah- A Hebrew term appearing frequently in the Psalms, signifying a pause for reflection, contemplation, and deeper spiritual awareness. In the context of awakening, it represents intentional moments to absorb divine revelation, allow truth to settle deeply into one's spirit, and create space for transformation beyond intellectual understanding. These sacred pauses invite readers to move from mere comprehension to personal encounter with the reality being described.

Shalom- More than the absence of conflict, shalom represents completeness, wholeness, and well-being in every area of life—spiritual, physical, emotional, and relational. This deep, abiding peace comes from knowing we are in Christ and He is in us, serving as a gateway to ascension experiences. (Philippians 4:7)

"This Is That"- The prophetic recognition when Heaven's blueprints, previously glimpsed through dreams, visions, or prophetic words, suddenly materialize in earthly experience. These moments of clarity validate spiritual experiences, confirm God's intimate involvement in our lives, and strengthen our faith in His perfect timing. (Acts 2:16)

Theosis- The journey of union with God, awakening to what has always been true about our divine nature in Christ. This concept, deeply explored by early Church Fathers, reveals that our origin isn't limited to time and space but is anchored in the Lamb slain before the foundation of the world. (2 Peter 1:4; Revelation 13:8)

Trinitarian Breathing- A spiritual practice of conscious breathing that aligns our awareness with the Triune God. As we inhale, we receive the Father's love, Son's grace, and Spirit's power; as we exhale, we release fear, performance, and earthly limitations. This simple act becomes a gateway to heavenly realms. (Genesis 2:7; Psalm 150:6)

Zōē- Greek word for the uncreated, divine life of God Himself—not just biological life (bios) or soul life (psuche). The supernatural, eternal life of God that believers possess now through Christ. Understanding zōē transforms our perception from seeing eternal life as a future reward to a present reality we live from. (John 10:10)

ABOUT THE AUTHORS

Bryan Elliott is an author, engineer, entrepreneur, and CEO of **Flō Energy Solutions Inc.**, operating across North America. His transformation from intellectual engineer to **kingdom-minded business leader** is chronicled in his earlier works, *More Than Gold* and *As in Heaven*, and culminates in *Ascension – Living Beyond Limits*. Bryan holds multiple technology patents, has founded several innovative companies, and serves on numerous corporate and nonprofit boards. As co-founder of **M46 Ministries** and **Bee Me Kidz**—a charity empowering children and families—he combines **spiritual awakening** with strategic leadership to bring **heavenly solutions** to real-world challenges. Bryan's unique ability to bridge the **marketplace and the supernatural** equips others to live from a place of **kingdom authority** and purpose.

Chantal Fowler is a prophetic voice and spiritual mentor known for her profound sensitivity to the **heavenly realm**. Born and raised on Canada's East Coast, Chantal has walked in deep **spiritual discernment** since childhood. After over 12 years as a worship leader at a House of Prayer, she joined Flō in 2016, where she now serves as Director of **Spiritual Operations**. Chantal is a pioneer in **marketplace ministry**, integrating prayer, **prophetic insight**, and **divine wisdom** into business environments. Her gift for turning spiritual encounters into practical action has helped countless individuals and organizations align with the **frequency of Heaven**. She empowers others to engage with God's presence and live from their seated position in Christ.

Together, Bryan and Chantal embody the convergence of the **analytical and the intuitive**, the **business world and the prayer room**, united by their passion for Jesus and the advancement of the **kingdom of Heaven** on earth.

What if your deepest pain could become your greatest purpose?

At **M46 Ministries**, we believe that nothing is wasted, and nothing is lost-in the hands of a redemptive God. Born from a powerful story of tragedy and transformation, M46 Ministries exists to help you walk in Kingdom identity, restore what's been broken, and bring heaven to earth right where you are.

 FREE BOOKS

 PODCASTS

 KINGDOM RESOURCES

Start your journey of healing and purpose today.

 Visit **M46Ministries**.com

Because God is still writing your story.

Personal stories. Biblical truth. Kingdom living.

Join Bryan, Bryn, and Matt as they bring *As In Heaven* to life, inviting you to live out heaven on earth through Christ.

Listen now at m46ministries.com/podcast

Or wherever you get your podcasts.

Hope has a voice. Come hear it.

Now Available

What if spiritual transformation isn't about becoming someone new but remembering who you've always been in Christ?

In AWAKENING: Restorative Metanoia, lay down the weight of religious striving and awaken to your redeemed innocence, divine union, and eternal identity. Drawing on personal stories, Greek word studies, and early Church wisdom, this book offers a freeing, hope-filled alternative to fear-based faith.

If you've ever longed for something deeper, consider this your invitation to come home.

A Story of loss, love, and Kingdom redemption.

When Bryan's daughter Abbe was tragically taken
from this world, God began to reveal a purpose far
greater than pain.
More Than Gold invites you into a journey of grief
and grace, where Jesus turns death into life and
suffering into glory.

**If you've ever wondered if God can redeem
your darkest moments, this book is for you.**

**Get your copy or read free at
m46ministries.com/books**

The story Satan tried to silence,
but God redeemed.

Addiction. Abuse. Rape. Murder.
Bryn S. Elliott lived through it all- and wanted to die.
But Jesus met her in the ashes and rewrote her story.
This powerful two-part book reveals Bryn's gripping jour-
ney from trauma to transformation and invites you to find
the same healing through a surrendered life with Jesus.

**A surrendered life may not be easy, but it will
always be worth it.**

Read her story. Start yours.
m46ministries.com/books